A Collection of Essays, Poems, and Meditations

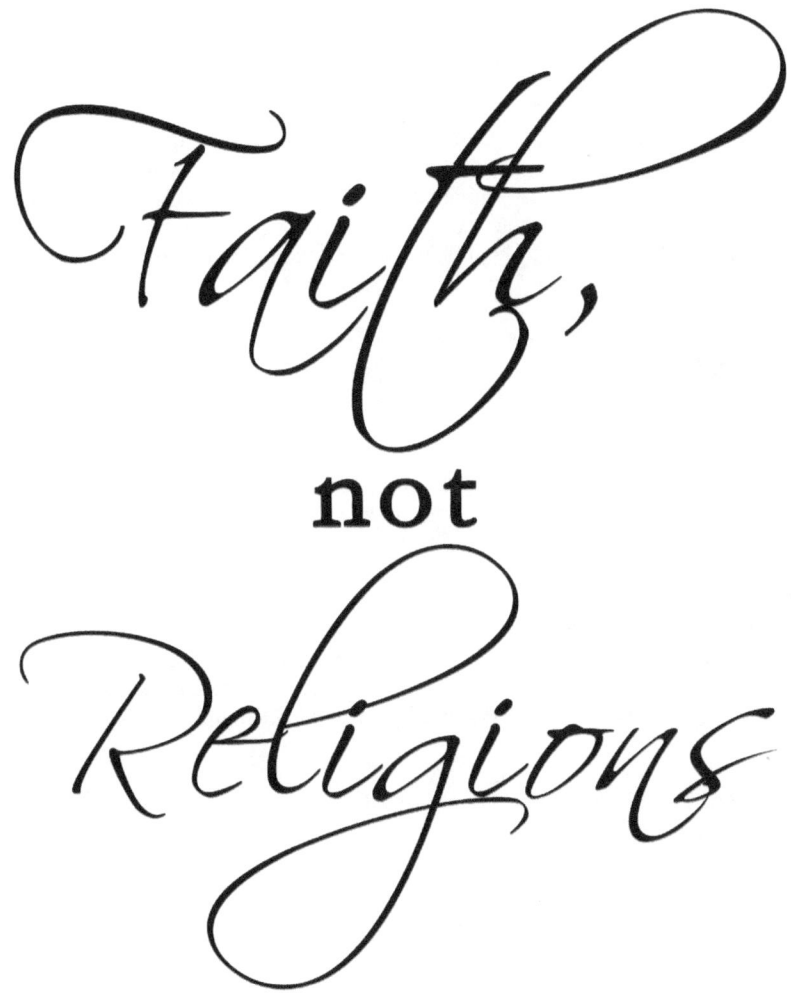

Faith, not Religions

Chatha Akbar Ghulam

Copyright © 2004, 2012, 2019 Chatha Ghulam

All rights reserved. No part of this publication may be reproduced, distributed, or transmitted in any form or by any means, including photocopying, recording, or other electronic or mechanical methods, without the prior written permission of the publisher, except in the case of brief quotations embodied in critical reviews and certain other noncommercial uses permitted by copyright law. For permission requests, write to the publisher, addressed "Attention: Permissions Coordinator," at the address below.

Zeta Publishing, Inc
3850 SE 58th Ave
Ocala, FL 34480
www.zetapublishing.com

This is a work of fiction. All of the characters, names, incidents, organizations, and dialogue in this novel are either the products of the author's imagination or are used fictitiously.

Ordering Information:
Quantity sales. Special discounts are available on quantity purchases by corporations, associations, and others. For details, contact the publisher at the address above.
Orders by U.S. trade bookstores and wholesalers. Please contact Zeta Publishing: Tel: (352) 694-2553; Fax: (352) 694-1791 or visit www.zetapublishing.com

First published by iUniverse in 2004 & 2012

Rev. Date: 1/24/2019

ISBN: 978-1-7335084-8-3 (sc)
ISBN: 978-1-7335084-9-0 (e)

Library of Congress: 2018968366
Printed in the United States of America

Dedicated to all free thinkers and, religiously oppressed persons around the globe.

ACKNOWLEDGMENT

Inspired by Punjabi mystic poets
Bulleh Shah
Madho Lal Shah Hussain
Sultan Bahoo
And
Khawja Fareed.

CONTENTS

FORWARD
INTRODUCTION
THE GOD
THE RELIGIOUS TERRORISM
THE ISLAMIC TERRORISM
UNAVOIDABLE SECTARIAN VIOLENCE IN ISLAM
THE UNIVERSAL MYSTICISM
TRADITIONS, CUSTOMS AND HOMELANDS
IN SEARCH OF THE GOD
MONISM AND MY GOD
THE GOD AND WARS
THE GOD'S REWARD AND PUNISHMENT
THE CREATOR OF TIME
THE GOD AND THE CEREMONIAL PRAYERS
THE GOD AND MORALITIES
THE PROTECTOR
THE MERCIFUL
THE GOD AND CIVILIZATIONS
THE GOD OF HUMANS
THE GOD AND HUMAN WISHES
THE GOD AND DIETIES
THE GOD AND JUSTICE
LIFE AND DEATH
LIBERALISM VERSUS FUNDAMENTALISM
THE CHANGING WORLD
THE NECESSITIES OF HUMAN LIFE
FREEDOM
THE QUEST FOR PEACE
TO BE A HUMAN
MAJORITY VS MINORITY
IN THE NAME OF GOD
THE DAY OF JUDGMENT
THE CHRIST YOU BELIEVE
I PRAYED TO THE GOD

WISDOM VS IGNORANCE
HUMANS AND ANIMALS
WHY PRIESTS, MONKS, NUNS DO NOT MARRY
EXPECTING MIRACLES
IS THE GOD UNJUST?
THE GOD IS JUST
FAITH VS RELIGIONS
RELIGION VS RELIGIONS
THE GOD AND ATTACHMENTS
I WISH
LAWFUL VICES
MORALE BOOSTING
GIVE AND TAKE OF SINS
"THANKS GOD"
COLLECTIVENESS AND FAITH
THE RETREATING RELIGIONS AND TRADITIONS
LOVE VS HATRED
THE GOD GIVEN
UNIVERSAL HARMONIES
TO MYSELF
IF I WERE
THE CHARM OF OBEDIENCE
SELFISHNESS (AN EXPLANATION)
AN OUTLAW FACES THE DAY OF JUDGMENT
SO WHAT
YEARNINGS OF A SOUL
DOES NOT RECOGNIZE THE GOD
RECOGNIZES THE GOD
THE CREATOR OF THE UNIVERSE
MINISTERS, JINN AND DEVILS
LET US SAY LOVE PRAYERS
DEPRESSION
HEAVEN AND HELL
SOME THOUGHTS AND OBSERVATIONS

To unite in the name of any religion,
To unite in the name of any nation,
To unite in the name of any region,
To unite in the name of cooperation,
Many claim, it as in the name of God,
Definitely not, it is definitely not,
All it is, but for any selfish cause,
To unite to prosper, or for any mistaken path,
Unite to struggle for the justice's sake,
To heighten the love and lower the hate,
Praise the God who blessed us with values great,
To defeat the evil -- every good is humane.

FORWARD

People either believe in religious God or Gods, or do not believe at all. Some religious people might even believe in a God or Gods of their wishes and likings, not a One True God. The God created humans, but some humans create their own God or Gods which they claim have special manners, prayers, books, and also special personalities and deities.

The God who created humans has nothing to do with such specialties and preferences. In this book the name of God is written without any additions or conditions. All sensible humans know what humanism is and what good human values are, so nothing additional and nothing inconsistent with humanism is mentioned or preached.

THE GOD

This God or that God,
Of turban's or the cap's God,
Of religion's or the priest's God,
Of West's or the East's God,
Which God, or whose God,
Not believe, or choose God,
Temple's God or minaret's God,
Not of free, but hostage's God,
Not certain, but uncertain God,
Of insane, not of sane God,
Only if God is The God,
Is God not this or that God.

INTRODUCTION

Friends, I am a farmer from the Punjab Pakistan. Not a learned person or scholar. I never visited libraries and never attended meetings of scholarly persons. I have never been abroad before 2012 when I came to USA to take asylum. Thanks to God for blessing me with a strong faith in Him.

I underwent a natural process not influenced by any person. I do not claim to be a special human and I believe in The God of all humans. I do not claim any special attachments with The God.

I also do not accept claims of people having a special attachment with The God, which other humans may or may not have or achieve. The God of humans basically created all humans equal.

I am not a professional or experienced writer and I never thought I could be one. In 2001 I joined some study groups and through the discussion of "faith" enjoyed the first ever outlet for my thoughts.

I am not a religious preacher. I only preach "faith" in One God. The God …and that is all.

I AM YOUR FRIEND ALSO

May not be of your skin,
May not be of your nation,
May not be of your language,
May not be of your standards,

Yet I can live as you live,
Yet I can sing as you sing,
Can love your art and ways of life,
The land you live in, or any sight,

I can join you in sad and glad,
Can share your hopes and wear, as you are clad,
Can join you in prayers where you pray,
Though I shall say silently what I have to say,

The God I pray is your God also,
May be more yours than mine,
The God of universe and mankind, also,
I am your friend.

I can join you to defend the just,
If you are to help weak or oppressed,
But if I happen to meet others,
If they claim to behave as human brothers,

I can be very easily inspired,
No restraints shall then I abide,
I shall embrace and say to them, also,
I am your friend.

THE GOD

Creator of the universe-Worthy of all praises -- The Mighty…The God is one, does not share power with any one; He is the only supreme. Only the God is to be believed; only the God is worthy of deserving our faith. The God of universe is not God of any particular-faith, race or group of people claiming superiority over others. These are charges against God which need to be vindicated, though God is not affected because he is supreme.

The God created mankind of a nature most liked by Himself; the nature which is extremely good, the good which you all know. The God created mankind of one common nature. The God likes to be praised, does not authorize anyone to force others to follow his way of prayers. We all know the manners of obedience; prayers cannot be said by crawling. No one should say prayers in a language in which he or she is not fluent. Feelings should be expressed in any language or silently.

The whole of mankind is born and dies. The God can do whatever He wants and certainly doesn't do injustice to anyone. The God will not hold responsible any person for not believing in anyone except The God. To believe in The God is natural, and nothing is more natural. A person is born in nature, not belonging to any area, race, linguistic or ethical group. One is often told by others to belong to such and such group, to adopt the likings and hatreds and selfishness that that group endorses. But the persons having wisdom and intellect are exceptions. These are the persons loved by God because only they have pure faith. If you put a newborn baby in another community, he or she will adopt the likings and disliking of that community, even when feeling affection for the acting parents.

Death materially equalizes all who die leaving behind all affiliations contracted during life. Humans attempt in vain to make some difference by performing ceremonies as dictated by our clerics, by military parades, or by erecting monuments and tombs. Only God can and will make a difference, rewarding the good and punishing the evil.

The people of wisdom recognize the good and evil the world over from the beginning of mankind to the present. God created mankind to be good, allows to be exposed to evil. Therefore, there is a reward for those who remain good and punishment for those who are lured by evil forces. A person in the wilderness, who is very hungry and shares his piece of bread with another person, is doing good. But why? This is because of God-given good nature. If a person does well to his family, community, or any other in the name of God, he is rewarded by God. To what extent, one doesn't know except God. A believer is the best and most steadfast good-doer. He or she remains on the straight path in any condition or circumstance. A disbeliever may change his good intention in crises, but a believer would not.

BE AWARE, AN OUTLAW IS AT LARGE

Though not bad mannered, though not a looter,
Though not wicked, though not a killer,
Yet he is treacherous, yet he is a swindler,
He may rob you of the most precious holding,
Your religious complacency, your holy belonging,
Be aware of him as he is a devil daring,
As he might be finished by brave persons,
And they take themselves guards of heavens.
He says he would not accept any born seniority,
Who-so-ever and which-so-ever might be authority,
He says, would the God damn other's children?
As when or were to be born may not be their concern,
He says he would take to task some or all,
Would face, each community large or small,
He says that all holy laws are man-made,
Which de-equalize the humans on any base,
How can religions survive if all are equal?
Be aware as he is a threat to their survival.

THE RELIGIOUS TERRORISM

The claim of supremacy in religion, race and language breeds terrorism. The God of the universe is the God of mankind and not God of any ethical group. But the groups are much too self-righteous and believe that the God is on their side. Every group cherishes the belief that the God has given them special preference over others. The preferences claimed are in respect of holy personalities, saints, books, the way and language in which they worship. They think that everything which belongs to their cult is superior, so the others should follow. Moreover, that their cult will predominate in this world and will be rewarded in the everlasting world after death and re-creation.

Such desires of supremacy and self-righteousness breed hatred and consequently terrorism.

[It seems that the idea is… 'Our rivals have been claiming superiority. Now we have gained power. Now we are superior and have our revered instead of theirs. They have been undermining our sermons and way of worship; now we do theirs. We have been suffering at their hands; now we shall punish them. They have been doing injustice to us but, we do justice because, we are right, and they are wrong!'…]

Each person has his self-righteousness with him. He is pleased when he hears the good qualities of everything that belongs to him and is angry when hearing negative remarks. The spiritual traits which are attributed to these personalities are held in the highest possible esteem. This causes deep-rooted divisions. All praises are for the God and the God only, but most humans are not pleased to listen to this exclusively. He the God of whole mankind does not satisfy their self-righteousness.

The self-righteousness can be identified and can be eliminated through wisdom. A true believer in the God has this wisdom and, capable of upholding the best moral and human values in a situation or circumstance in which a non-believer can fail.

Self-righteousness causes injustice, anger, revolt, hostilities, hate and wars. These wars are not in the name of the God, but only to satisfy rigid beliefs. Then there are cruelties, terrorism…

War is justified if it is to protect and help lawfulness, the wronged and the oppressed. Self-protection if attacked is a basic right. Believers in the God understand better these justifications.

HOLD A WHILE

Don't kill me, this is inhuman,
To torture in such a way is un-Godly,
To pierce the flesh, to break the bones,
To insert the bullets, to cut the throat,
Of anyone who hasn't done any harm to you,
Who neither attempted nor intended
To kill any of you is sheer brutality.

Listen to me and hold a while.
I'm not who you take me for,
Believe me, I'm not your enemy.
Yes, I was born among those.
I know you and they are each other's foes.
This is not my fault, the God, the God,
This is not my choice, no, absolutely.

Listen to me and hold a while,
Don't you have sisters and brothers?
Mothers, fathers and children you love?
Friends and dears, those who will miss you much
And feel a great agony if any one of you
Is caught in such a situation as I?
Will they not wail and sigh?
On such a death if you are to die?

Listen to me and hold a while,
It seems that you don't want to heed.
You are bent to do what you intend.
Be not in haste, are you getting late?
Allow me a few moments to pray to the God,
The God of mankind, God of Arabs and Jews,
The God of all, Christian, Muslims, Hindus.
Oh! My God, only you are the God, the God.

ISLAMIC TERRORISM

Others have much more civilized their religions and Muslims need to, otherwise; they are and, would continue to be trouble makers in the world. Life is not easy in Islamic countries/communities for those who are aware of human rights. Beside this when Muslims want to practice and, act upon their so-called true religion they create big problems for so-called infidels. There are such so-called holy commandments in Islamic doctrine for true Muslims which, if acted upon are totally intolerable/inacceptable in civilized societies.

No Muslim scholar moderate or not can explain to make those commandments acceptable. Many would claim that they can but, can not answer questions by fact checking persons like me. Yes, they can not. Hypocrisy to such extant can not be concealed.

Others practice their faith truly or not as per respective doctrines or stories which, can not be fully ascertained in history. Life of Islamic prophet is not only clear in history; Muslims also believe that, prophet did set perfect examples for every true Muslim covering all phases, situations, steps of life to follow. These so-called perfect examples are also supported by many so-called holy sayings called, "Hadiths". Why many Muslims do not practice those perfect examples? All of them do believe that the prophet was the best person/prophet for ever and, no one can equal him in any sense. They want or at least wish to kill any person who, dares to challenge such reverence. Those so-called perfect examples are also totally impracticable in civilized world. Would any Muslim say, "those perfect examples can be modified"? No, being a Muslim he/she can not say. Then what is the solution?

Yes, the only possible solution for Muslims is to believe and not practice which, many may be already doing. Why they don't acknowledge? Because by acknowledging they wouldn't be Muslims any more so, they would not want , like, dare to. They can not even think about such a freedom. There can be so-called freedom of thought or proclaimed but, real freedom of thought is contrary/opposite to especially Islamic belief though, I do not believe in any religion.

There are specific, clear laws/codes to be implemented on individual, society and also on government level. Other religions have not such covering and also clarity of so-called holy laws so, they can have an excuse. Should not Muslims want and, also strive for implementation of those holy/sacred laws? Yes, All of them do believe the laws are holy and sacred.

If that impracticable is made practicable in this modern world, civilized society would definitely call, "TERRORISM" though, many for political and strategic reasons would not name it, "ISLAMIC". Certainly, those now seemingly impracticable were practiced in so-called holy times of the prophet and subsequent so-called holy caliphs. ISIS and Taliban tried to implement/follow those laws but many Muslims and especially governments of Islamic countries denied and, continue to deny their Islamic authenticity for self interest. What is authentic, real, true if not this/that? Would any Islamic scholar explain, tell, define? Certainly none and, no one can. Truth is much harsh and horrible.

Mystical poet Bulleh Shah says,
"Exposing truth would cause a huge fire so, be safe by telling lies."

UNAVOIDABLE SECTARIAN VIOLENCE IN ISLAM

There was sectarian violence in other religions in history but, in recent times it seems to be almost over. As compared to other religions Islam experienced much worse violence, is continuing and, certainly would continue. States may fail to control the situation and, in such a situation it would get much horrible just like Iraq, Syria and even worse than that. Why it can not be over in modern/civilized times? Here are some important facts!

Let us first discuss much smaller factions like Ahmadis, etc.; who would be eliminated if anytime law and order fails because, they are considered heretics so can not be tolerated under Islamic sharia. Muslims don't compromise on finality of Islamic prophet so, Ahmadis etc. have already been declared non-Muslims as per state laws in countries like Pakistan, where they are in considerable numbers. They are prohibited to perform Haj/annual pilgrimage to Mecca/Medina in Saudi Arabia though, they claim to be true Muslims.

Now let us go through history of Islam and, know about real, big, dangerous, unavoidable problem.

When Islamic prophet formed a state, laws were required so, he received orders from Allah or, dealt with situations according to requirements. Certainly, his dealing or verdicts are taken sacred to highest level by Muslims. To run a state harsh laws, orders were need of time in that medieval Arab society.

Conversion from Islam punishable by death;

Rebellion against Islamic regime or involvement in any conspiracy against, punishable by death of males (able to fight), confiscation of property and assets, taking women as sex slaves, etc. etc. Approximately above ten were considered as able to fight; sick/disable were exempted. Islamic prophet also had 6,7 or more sex slaves (not married).

Almost same rules were applied when Islamic forces happen to conquer any area.

Sharia laws such as stoning to death, cutting of hands, lashing for out of marriage sex and drinking (such lashing might result in death).

Death for insulting prophet or Islam etc.

When Islamic prophet was on his death bed, struggle to grab the power was natural. In such struggle many even didn't attend funeral of their prophet and; as a result who were opposed to dominance of direct prophet's family, succeeded in getting the power without prophet's consent. They continuously downgraded the prophet's family taking them as possible adversaries. There happened a revolt against third caliph of Islam, he was killed and, as a result the only son in-law of prophet became 4th caliph. 2nd caliph was also assassinated by his slave for mistreatment. 3rd caliph was from Umayyad tribe. None of this tribe accepted Islam except him until, city of Mecca was captured by Islamic Army led by prophet and, all have to be Muslims or killed; so, all of them accepted Islam. Arch rival of prophet Abu-Sufyan was also leader of this tribe and, under his leadership battles were fought against Islam/Muhammad. 3rd caliph during his rule rewarded greatly his tribe so, Muawiyah son of Abu-Sufyan was governor of Syria when Ali who was also cousin of Muhammad became 4th caliph. All of Hashemite , the tribe of Muhammad were among the first Muslims. Muhammad had only one daughter called Fatima. She was married with Ali.

Muawiyah denied to accept Ali as caliph so, there was a clash. Thousands from both sides embraced so-called martyrdom but clash remained in-decisive. Aisha wife of Muhammad (married at the age of nine) who was daughter of 1st caliph Abu-Bakar also took side with Muawiyah against Ali; an other big battle was fought between her and Ali, thousands embraced so-called martyrdom on both sides. Ali was killed by an other rebellious group who were opposed to both groups fighting for rule. Hassan son of Ali took over as the leader but, Muawiyah spared no time to avail the opportunity. He marched to grab the power and, was successful in getting full control of Islamic empire. It may be said as irony of fate or, upsetting that, Umayyad which was rival tribe of Hashemite (tribe of Muhammad) took over the rule of Islamic empire. Abu-Sufyan vs. Muhammad; Muawiyah (son of Abu-Sufian) vs. Ali and, then Yazid (son of Muawiyah) vs. Hussain (son of Ali). Hussain and many family members were killed in Karbala now city of Iraq and, women/children imprisoned by Yazidi forces. Shiite Muslims observe that tragedy by weeping, beating their chests.

Muawiyah as a founder of Umayyad dynasty got a fatwa (religious decree) from clergies that, Ali (cousin and son-in-law of Muhammad) was a rebel so, should be cursed as such. Umayyad dynasty ruled for about a century and, during that period Ali was cursed in every mosque (including holiest) in weekly Jummah (Friday) sermons by prayer leaders. Certainly they also believed that, Yazid son of Muawiyah was right to brutally punish family of Hussain son of Ali. Many well known Islamic conquerors happened to be generals of Umayyad dynasty including those who conquered Spain and Sind (India). When Umayyad dynasty fell, most of them were killed. That was an extended tribe. Their graves were also destroyed.

Almost 80% of Muslims are Sunni. They hold 1st caliph as holiest person after prophet and so, 2nd, 3rd, 4th, etc.. They also believe that Aisha and Muawiyah are among the holiest personalities of Islam. Most Sunni respect Ali and family more than Muawiyah but, believe that Muawiyah is also sacred. Holding opposite to, or enemies of each other sacred is certainly non-sense but, most Muslims are cherishing this non-sense whole heartedly. Almost all terrorists of recent times belong to Sunni/Salafi sect of Islam. Sunni/Salafi sect believes that Shiite are heretics. Salafi/Sunni also consider some Sunni sections as not true Muslims and, willing to commit violence against them also.

Shiite for obvious reasons hate 1st, 2nd, 3rd caliphate and curse Aisha, Muawiyah etc. as most evil persons. They believe Ali was the most legitimate successor of Muhammad which opposing group prevented to happen. They also believe that tragedy of Karbala in which family of Hussain (grandson of Muhammad) was horribly dealt with, was the result of ill-legitimate usurping of power after Muhammad died.

Details of history can not be mentioned here but, the facts are undeniable. So, there are not merely differences in beliefs which, can be reconciled or tolerated. It is something much complicated, much hateful, much horrible to be avoided. To be unaware of the facts or ignoring them is beneficial for opposing sections. Especially Shiite ignore because, Sunni are in great majority all over the world. No section of Islam is as violent as Sunni/ Wahhabi though extremism exists in all sections which, can be violent at any time.

THE UNIVERSAL MYSTICISM

The God of the universe, the God of mankind is the God of love. Parents' love for their baby is natural. Being the producers of that baby, they love the child. The God is the creator of mankind and loves the creation. In rare cases the parents' love can waive, but the God's love is eternal. The God wants humans to promote love among themselves. Only for this cause should there be justice, liberty and human rights.

Please look into this mysticism. (Love for the God)

Sultan Bahoo says,
"I want to do away with eemaan (the faith of a Muslim), as everybody prays for the survival of eemaan in himself, I seek the survival of my ishq" (profound love).

"Ashiqs (lovers) say prayers of love, in which there is no word."

"Those who say pure prayer do not move or shiver their tongue" (being silent).

"Mind and thought have no place in love of the God. Also mullah (Muslim clerk), pundit, joshi (Hindu clerk) cannot reach there, even the recitation of The Koran (Muslim holy book) will not do."

"Ghous, qutab (higher ranks of Muslim saints) cannot reach that place where ashiqs can. The lovers can reach the destination where the ghouses cannot go around."

"Tummay (herbal unpalatable) cannot be turboose (watermelon), by taking them to Mecca (holiest place), as the black crows cannot be whitened."

Bulleh Shah, a fugitive of prevailing norms says,
"Throw the prayers in a furnace, paste mud on fasts, and spray black over kalma (the first necessary words to be recited by a Muslim. Those who don't believe or recite are not Muslims).

Bulleh Shah, your beloved is within you (in your heart), mankind is strayed aimlessly."

"Shariah (Muslim code of manners, prayers, says,
'Go to mullah and learn the manners. Ishq says, one word is sufficient... leave all the books."

"Oh Bulleh, let us go to a place where all are blind, so that no one knows our caste and no one believes. (He was Syed, progeny of Muslim prophet, religiously esteemed caste.) He believes in equality of mankind.

"Demolish mender (Hindus place of worship), demolish mosque. Do not demolish (break) human heart, herein the God resides."

Madho Lal Shah Hussein says,
"Qazi, mullah advises, those who know more (learned clergies) are telling us to adopt the way. Ishq has nothing to do with ways. I love the beloved" (the God).

Madho Lal (a Hindu by name) was a friend of Shah Hussein. Shah Hussein never asked Madho Lal to change his name or religion ceremonially. He loved his friend so much that he and Madho Lal joined names. Both were buried side by side according as per his will. Now-a-days it is very difficult to bury a Madho Lal in a Muslim graveyard. Even the army cannot do it. There will be a holy war to prevent this. People say that Madho Lal was actually a believer in his heart.

Khawja Fareed,

I abandoned five times Islamic prayers, dogs of religions bark a lot, don't know about depth of meditation/thinking.

Chatha Ghulam

This is just a presentation from Punjabi mystic poets, which I liked to present. I think these poets tried to speak the truth in defiance of prevailing hypocrisies. Some people might say, "This is just nonsense." Others believe they were saints and provided a link between the God and humanity. People pray in the mosques adjacent to their tombs. I wonder how these mystics can be misinterpreted. I think their religion cannot be labeled, and to me there is much similarity of thought.

TRADITIONS, CUSTOMS AND HOMELANDS

The God is universal and I am preaching universalism. But by this I don't negate the identities regarding nations, languages, castes, regions, traditions and customs. I insist that the God is one, "Almighty," and on universal justice and equality. This doesn't hurt anyone. I have nothing more. Love is the message.

Once in my childhood I was listening to a debate (though not a serious one) in my village, Punjab, Pakistan, regarding superiority of castes. One of my uncles said, "The God made two castes, including ours." Then the people said to the God, "Where do we stand?" "Shall we have no caste?" The God ordered the angels, "Go and give them also some names." Our caste is made by the God and yours by the angels, so we stand superior. The men and the children, including me, having this superior caste were very pleased with these remarks. There was clapping and laughing, as we had won the debate.

The story pleased me and I wished it were true. Now I am ashamed of myself for having developed that wish. Mankind goes on with such wishes. With the passage of time these wishes are intermixed with beliefs and gain much solid ground. When we say, "In those golden times," it takes us into an imaginary world. In fact, there aren't any golden times and no bad times. There is good and evil in all times. Excluding such like wishes, all traditions and customs are good. All nations, all languages, all castes, and all races are good, and there is no harm in maintaining their own identities in the God's universe.

I belong to a native Punjabi landowner's caste. My caste is a part of my name and this is a symbol of identity, not a symbol of pride or differentiation from others. I want to learn all languages of the world to easily communicate with all kinds of people, but it is not possible. I want to be among the different civilizations of the world, but this is difficult for me. I want to freely roam about in mosques, churches, mandars, gurdwaras, temples etc.

Bulleh Shah, a Punjabi mystic poet, says, "Forsake the enmities, and make no noise. These Turks (Mughals, Muslim nobles) and Hindus are not separate. He (The God) possesses all."

I don't need any reference books for authority or material. I only want to express my inner self, my heart and mind. The love of homeland is very natural. I also love my homeland, local music, language, customs and traditions, which are not against human values. For example, I don't like the sectarian march in Ireland which reminds others that they were defeated, and thereby hurting their feelings. Even the animals love their homes and the areas where they live. I observed the horses and the dogs not willing to leave their previous dwellings unless they were forced to leave. I love the weather, trees, birds, and everything of my homeland. I shall not feel happy even to change the area of my dwelling within the country…but, people do migrate to other regions for the sake of safety, livelihood, and better prospects. If I find anyone having similarity of thoughts, I shall love him or her above all the affiliations I have. To promote this thought is my sincere desire, and for this cause, affiliations don't matter.

YOUR GOD

What? You have your supreme God,
And will not believe in mine?
Yours is the true God and mine is not?
Not you, but I have to believe in thine?
Does your God hate me and loves you?
Do you belong to Him and He to you?
And you will not let me pray, if I want to,
But in solitude I shall definitely break through.
I shall say I haven't done if you are angry.
What? My prayers qualify not the standard glory?
I am alone and it requires a group or company,
Oh, yes, God is yours and to pray, I am a silly.
Oh, Lord I have to offer you a sincere heart,
Though broken by your people's stabbing taunts,
I shall pray to you all times in all my life,
No matter, if not allowed in worship spots.

IN SEARCH OF THE GOD

I believe that the God created the universe and everything. The God gave mankind the sensibility to discern between good and evil, therefore be liable to rewards and punishment. This is only the base of my belief and nothing more.

Bulleh Shah (a Punjabi mystic poet) says, "Oh Bulleh, you are the ashiq (profound lover) of the God, therefore millions of condemnations for you," (by the people). They call you, "kafir, kafir, and "(non-believer) You say, "Yes, yes," (I am).

"No one can be a true lover (of God) without being a real kafir (non-Muslim)."

In the holy books of Jews, Christians and Muslims there are personalities, places and stories alike and not alike. These things do not matter. The main purpose is to guide mankind, and I think there are many misrepresentations. Hindus have their many deities sharing powers. I believe in the Almighty One God. However, there isn't any harm if they continue telling stories as the Greeks and Italians do. Every nation or region has its own traditions and customs. These are not objectionable if they are not against the basic human rights or do not harm others' feelings. The high human values are much appreciated, liked and rewarded by the God.

A few centuries ago Australia, the Americas and several other parts of the world were unknown to the people of the known world. The natives of these regions didn't know and couldn't know about religions that were practiced in the rest of the world. Were they to be blamed for that? God forbid! The God did not give them the opportunity to join one of the best religions? Is the God so unfair and unjust? No, I do not believe in such a God, sending messengers to one part of the world and not to another depriving them of the knowledge. The people should have been given guidance by the God. Anyone seeking the truth or searching for the God is sure to find out. Is not the God omnipresent? Yes, the God is, and He asks the humans, "If there is anybody who wants to search for me, I am much closer to you than anyone else can be." Of course, sincerity is a pre-requisite for receiving his guidance.

Jewish, Christian, Muslim, Hindu, Buddhist, Sikh people pray to a God or the deities of the religion they choose. These are chosen for various reasons – because they are the religions of their forefathers, or because of the land or region they live. They also seek the guidance from the God under the preconditions of their cherished religion.

To lay preconditions before the Almighty is insensible and unjust. Just be human and not Christian, Jew, Muslim, Hindu, Buddhist, Sikh or German, Russian, American, Spanish, Arabian, Indian, black or white. The God created humans. We humans adopted all these divisions, when we grew up. Our self-righteousness bred prejudice and bigotry.

I believe that if a person who is sensible enough, is willing to release himself from all the above mentioned divisions, and is totally sincere in searching for the God or seeking guidance, he is granted that which he seeks. It is most necessary to reach this point for guidance or inspiration from the God. This believer might be anyone or anywhere in the world. Surrendering entirely before the God and leaving obstinacy is a must. Once a person attains this goal, he is not only forgiven, but is loved by the God.

Only the God is most loving and the God loves mankind. Unlike religions, faith in the God is neither a heritage, nor an inheritance.
Whosoever spreads message of love, God given universal human values is messenger of God, angel visits not required.

A CHILD AND A FATHER

Oh father, my loving father, I have some questions in my mind,
You have been answering me, but now I am grown up,
And the complexities of life and nature confuse me much,
I have looked upon you for satisfaction and truth.

Oh father, why are there many disparities among humans?
Some live a rich life having much more than their just needs,
Some are denied bread though they embrace the disgrace of begging,
Why doesn't the God feed them and shelter the poor and weak?

Oh father, tell me why the earth quakes to demolish poor homes,
How helpless is he when his dears give up to fatal disease,
Somewhere drought threatens life and somewhere rain ruins hopes,
Many die under the scorching sun and many do not endure shivering cold.

Oh father, tell me why battles are fought and mighty crushes weak,
Many die and many cry and victory dances over death and blood,
Widows cry, mothers sigh, while fathers kneel down over dying sons,
Sorry father, it makes me very sad, and you say that the God is Merciful.

My son, my dear son, you are a good sensible child,
I hope the God will guide you as you seek the way to Him,
The God is Merciful and he loves those who feel mercy,
To solace you is my duty, but answers you ask I do not have.

Sooner or later everybody has to die and the rich also suffer,
To some the God gives tests and to some He gives a long rope,
Many times the God changes ups to downs and downs to ups,
Even then humans do not understand and share the devil's pride.

The devil teaches them to be proud of groups, religions and races,
They fight each other since the devil is the enemy of the God and humans,
The God's believers are not quarrelsome, but loving, as you are.
Pray to the God, my son, and know that the God cares for everyone.

MONISM AND MY GOD

The God knows each and every thing, which was, is and shall be. The God is neither he nor she, but only for our convenience in expression, we call Him He, having no beginning and no end. He created the universe. The God, who is almighty, omnipotent, omnipresent, and is aware of the minutest movements in it, neither is He an offspring of any, nor does He have any offspring. Only He is worthy of all praise. He neither sleeps nor tires. He cares for his each and every creation and doesn't forget. He knows what everybody speaks or has in his mind and heart. Only He knows the hidden, concealed and invisible. No one else has these qualities, nor does anyone share these with him. He surely listens and responds to everyone who calls or remembers him. This call should be direct and not shared by anyone as it is a clear belief that no one else is worthy of being called. If someone is deeply troubled…facing his own death, or that of a dear one, he is most likely to shake off his polytheistic belief. But when he is relieved, he returns to the belief that he had before and reasserts his pride of having a religion. Pride of any kind including that of piety (self-righteousness) is a great hindrance in the way to the God.

A true believer enjoys a satisfaction which others cannot. He/she believes that all events happen according to the God's will and God knows better. So he/she prays to the God, asks for his favors and doesn't complain. When gains something, praises the God for His benevolence. When loses something seeks the God's help…it may be sad or full of sorrow with weeping, but not agitating.

Once there was a God's man who would always say thanks to God. He lived outside a small village. In that village a boy, much loved by his parents and relatives, died. The villagers went to the man for consolation, praying and seeking explanation as to why the event happened. The man expressed his sympathy, but also said, "Thanks be to God." The villagers were very annoyed at his saying thanks to God and planned to teach him a lesson. The man used to go on a morning walk outside his hut. The villagers sat on the way planning to harm the man. On that day before the man reached the place where they were waiting, his foot twisted, causing severe pain. His disciples took him back to the hut. After waiting for some time, the villagers came to the hut and expressed sorrow at his injury. As he said thanks to God it happened. The villagers were much ashamed. They told him of their plan and asked him to forgive them for their ignorance. After that incident, they became his disciples.

A God's man was traveling in hot weather. He was barefoot. He complained to the God for not giving him a pair of shoes. While he was walking, he saw a man whose feet had accidentally been severed. The God's man was much repentant about his desire to have shoes and thanked God for his healthy complete body.

A person should be grateful to the God for having food, health, sincere friends, a loving spouse, obedient sons and daughters and all else that cannot be mentioned here. This is God's benevolence and not necessarily what he deserves. Be thankful to a person who helps you, but praise the God by whose will he came to your help and who made up his mind to help you. To seek the God's mercy and benevolence is a must. Nobody has a claim on the God, no matter how pious he is. All are God's blessings.

I have already written on one supreme nature which the God has given to mankind. For example, no civilization ever praised cruelty, disloyalty, unfaithfulness, lying or selfishness. No creation of the God is purposeless. Each creation has an assigned task. Even animals have the sense of loyalty, but being naturally inferior may prove cruel and selfish. They have no such values as humans have.

Love between humans is not guaranteed. The God created that love among them although in very rare cases even close relatives turn enemies to each other. Sometimes closest friends do more harm than fatal enemies. If a man enjoys these loves, he should be grateful to the God. The God wants mankind to love each other but only God's love for mankind is absolutely reliable. To seek the God's blessings in each and every relation, in each and every deed and at all times is a must.

Bulleh Shah says, "Hajis (pilgrims) go to Mecca. We shall go to Takhat Hazara (home town of the hero of a classical love story). Where the beloved lives, there is Kabbah (most holy place of Muslims). There you can see the four books (Zabboor (book of David), Torah, Bible, and Koran)."

DO YOU LISTEN?

Do you listen? You gods, gods of communities and groups,
Why do you divide mankind to hate and fight?
Why do you teach them to be cruel and to be proud?
Why don't you fight yourselves against each other?

To keep your existence, wars are a must,
To keep you in mind, pride is necessary,
Struggle hard lest mankind believes in one God,
Keep them deceived, you deceivers, lest you die.

I believe you don't listen and you are not the living gods.
This is the devil that befools mankind as he is their enemy,
He misleads selfish humans to create their own gods,
So they become misers, wicked… and betray each other's faith.

Oh the God! You help your believers, help in your name.
You are the protector, the merciful. Protect in your name.
The believers of gods threaten us not to speak your name,
They say that they can be merciless, and merciless they are.

THE GOD AND WARS

Irrationality in societies is the main hindrance in the way of wisdom and in the way to the God. The God's men can never be quarrelsome and obstinate. They are passive rather than aggressive. Obstinacy, irrationality, greed and pride of power have been causes of most wars in the history of mankind. One of the concerned groups is sure to have one of these vices. In many cases both the groups have no right reason to be at war. War is almost impossible among two or more just groups. If both the groups are of the right cause, why war? For the believers, they can benefit from their own beliefs, but should never encroach upon others. If they do so, are they then so-called believers?

Obstinacy and irrationality abide in the religions cherished by the people. In uncivilized societies (there are also uncivilized people in so called civilized communities), if one says there isn't any God, people may object, but will not take it seriously. But if one says there weren't a particular prophet, people may grow so furious that they may do anything. They don't consider that, how can there be a prophet if there isn't any God? They can tolerate someone abusing the God, but if one makes remarks about their cherished personalities a bit lower than their conception of that cherished personality, there is much anger and in some cases extreme consequence. Then they claim their actions are holy. Has the God anything to do with such holiness?

A human approach in all matters and to all events of past and present is necessary for a true believer of the God. A believer has the God's gifted eye (approach) to see all matters on pure humanitarian grounds.

I think, according to my knowledge of history, none of the parties in The Crusades were fighting holy war. These were also the wars among groups. None fought for the sake of the God. I don't find any act of holiness in the fighting between Pakistan and India, Palestine and Israel, or so-called Islamic wars in history. My heart is grieved over the gruesome cruelties committed at the time of partition of India in 1947, on both sides of the border, but none of the groups acknowledges the cruelties. Adolph Hitler is hated because he was an evil person. He committed atrocities against all mankind, particularly Jews. Hajjaj bin Yusuf is hated not only because he sent his forces to Sind (India) and Spain, but because he was a cruel man and was against humanity. Wars fought by the Muslim conquerors were not holy and were not at all for the God's sake.

There is a time to take the wars of the past among the groups as events of history and not as a base for practicing animosity or malice. When a group in power has been very unjust to another group and seeks justice when overcome or subdued by the other group, most often the help is denied. The believers of the God don't seek harsh revenge when they are in power. They are merciful and if they are not, they are not the believers.

Self-defense is everybody's right and war fought for this purpose is just, if not holy. The war fought to protect innocent people, to stop the cruelties, and to provide justice, is holy. And, if fought while having in mind that the God likes it, it is the noblest action one can take. The name of jihad has been so abused that I do not like to call this action jihad. Wickedness is wickedness and cruelty is cruelty and, being humans, we all know what these words mean. But biased groups change the definitions when they come to know who committed the offence and against whom it was committed. The God hates killing and cruelties. He does not judge who the aggressor is or who the defender is. He is the God of the universe, the God of humanity. He doesn't like the atrocities of one group against another, no matter which groups these are. I wish for everyone his own liberties. I wish love amongst mankind based on equality and justice.

A CHILD AND A MOTHER

My mother brought for me a history book,
She says, it is interesting to read and is very useful,
It contains many events of a thousand years ago,
Real stories about people of the world and wars also.

I read! What interesting people are in the ages old!
I enjoy their interesting ways of living and life,
They celebrate festivals, make love, sing and dance,
But, oh mom, they now appear with spears and swords,
Oh mom, they kill and pierce, they are so brutal,
I shall not read, and I don't like this at all!

Mother says, "It is so old, take it like fiction and continue."

There is the story of two brothers, their daughters and their sons,
Happily they live, not allowing others to overcome,
The brotherhood keeps them united against all foes,
They grow in numbers and attain millions score,
Oh mom, they are now each other's enemy and swords drawn,
Oh mom, so much blood, blood they share and I can't read on.

Mother says, "It happened a thousand years ago, and you need not worry."

In this chapter some good and wise nations live,
Working, trading and reaping the crops they sow,
Eating, wearing clothes and living as they like,
How to stand for prayers is the only dispute they have,
Oh mom, dispute, quarrel, scuffle, fight and war,
Oh mom, merciless, terrifying how can I read this all.

Mother says, "History can't be without wars...be not so sensitive my child."

Here the nations unite to protect their sacred creeds,
Both groups tempt those who have religious pride,
With shining swords they decide, who owns the holy sight,

Hopping horses and human blood will get them paradise,
Oh mom, see the zealots fight to kill or be killed,
Both kill for the noble cause…so, who is on the God's side?

Here the pride of nations, not of religions, scowls with glare,
Big forces, big nations, and for small they don't care,
Huge armories, huge armies, in millions they count,
In millions they die, in millions they kill, so are they great,
Great disasters, great explosions, oh mom, too much "great,"
Ah mom, terrible, horrible, tell me where the God lives.

Mother says, "Be not divided and disturbed, here I tell you the simple truth."

"My dear child, the God doesn't want humans to fight and quarrel,
He doesn't prefer any religion, race, nation, or any group,
He hates pride in humans which makes them each other's foe,
He is merciful equally to all humans and wants them to be so,
The devil, enemy of man and the God, tries to make this world dreadful,
And his followers assist him by being greedy, cruel and revengeful."

THE GOD'S REWARD AND PUNISHMENT

By the grace of God, the God of the universe rewards the good humans and not a particular group. He punishes evil doers but not those who disagree with any group. The best reward is the right guidance and belief which results in self-contentment and the worst is misguidance which results in discontentment and despair. The God surely gives guidance to whoever seeks it. The God's rewards and punishments are in this world and in the hereafter also. Only the God can do full justice to anyone and everybody.

Society (human beings) never gives complete suitable rewards or punishment to anyone as they don't have the capability. The God wants human beings to do justice according to their potential and knowledge. For example, one man killed one man and another killed three. Both are killers, but by the scale of cruelty, the first might receive more punishment than the second, so justice does not rely on numbers. If a man snatched bread from a hungry person, he might receive more punishment than one who has robbed millions.

Nobody knows who is lucky and who is unlucky. For example, there were two persons, one a rich man and he could eat all that he wanted. The second man was poor, so could only eat simple bread …hardly enough to feed himself. A year goes by. The first man was caught in a situation that he could not get anything to eat for the last five days of the year; the second got his feed for the full year. The first envied the second's fate. This is the God's justice that all humans cannot see, but the God's men believe in and remain contented.

A wise man said, "One who sees anything which he does not possess and after seeing did not develop a wish for that thing to be in his possession, has given that thing in charity for the God's sake." (These things may be a vehicle, building, territory, an army, power, or money…)

Try to understand the lines. Perhaps I shall not be able to explain them fully. This is a believer's contentment and also a scale for measuring real nobility; but only God can measure it. The noble man believes in the God's will and is ever pleased with his God. He believes that which God has given him is not only sufficient for him, but only that much is good for him. The scale of nobility is the point where a man loses his patience and wishes those things to be in his possession which he does not have. He is happy with his fate because the God decreed it. All these things are consumable and will be spent; even life itself is temporary and this period seems to man too short. He believes that only the God is worthy of handling the universe and each thing in it. The God is handling it very equitably so there is no complaint of any sort. This is content

Every individual member of humanity is himself humanity as he is the trustee of the God-given values. We call these human values human rights. A believer of the God understands and can interpret these values far better. As a believer, he can uphold and protect these values even at the risk of his life.

Spirituality is to act only for the God's sake, which should be unshared, only the God, only one God. The act should not be for a custom, tradition, including religious applause, appreciation, or any other gain. If there is any other purpose then this is not the God's sake. If any act is done for the God's sake, only then does the God reward and only then he measures the sincerity of that act. Sincerity matters - not the quantity, amounts or numbers of prayers, fasts, or alms. The God is not concerned about the so-called manners and procedures of religious groups. Only the God knows the intentions – good or bad.

LUCKY OR UNLUCKY?

Lucky is the person, who is enjoying life,
Who is he and who is she, who is that lucky?
One who eats well or wears well?
One who is rich enough, or one who just eats to live,
One who lives in a palace, or one in a hut,
One having sons and daughters, or one having none,
One who gains repute, or an unknown who dies,
Has a tomb on his grave, or unmarked it lays?

It is said that the lucky are born rich,
Worry nothing and smoothly they live,
Being envied by others satisfies them much,
Even then despair often gives them a bitter touch.

It is said that healthy ones are lucky,
They enjoy life better than the sick,
But also they fear the loss of their health,
And certainly, health only is not life itself.

The clergy says, he knows who are lucky,
Those who agree with him and don't dissent,
He guarantees for them the paradise of the God,
The place of eternal pleasures he reserves for them.

The people say, those who unite are lucky,
They gain strength to protect and exceed,
They threaten the weak and power they show,
Then to have a natural fall prouder they grow.

Are those lucky who live into old age?
They live longer but are feeble and frail,
Disfigured in shape, a burden for youth and young,
They also love life and love all that lives.

Lucky or unlucky I am, I don't know,
I haven't knowledge and power to compete or comprehend

Chatha Ghulam

My Lord, the Lord of the universe, I am yours and yours only,
So help me, guide me, and take me as a whole.

If you accept me, lucky or unlucky doesn't matter,
I feel then satisfied and am ever grateful,
The devil sometimes makes me feel that I am great,
Even then, forgive me my Lord, You are the merciful.

THE CREATOR OF TIME

By the name of Almighty the God, when was time started? When will it end? One certainly doesn't know and can't know. How vast this universe is! One cannot imagine and will not be able to imagine. Eternity can neither be proved nor defined, but it can be felt. The God's men do feel it.

For example – just for explanation – it is said that once upon a time there was a God's man. God sent his angel to tell him that the time of his death had approached. The God's man replied to the angel that he didn't want to die at that time. The angel then asked the God for further orders. The God said, "Tell him, that he can live as many years as he wants, but ask him the number of years." The angel again appeared before that man and delivered the message. The man asked the angel, "Is there a time limit in which I have to die?" The angel replied, "Death is a must for all the creations." The man replied, "Come, I am ready to die. That time will also approach, so better to die now and fulfill the God's will." Humans can feel eternity within themselves.

For further explanation, let me tell another story. This will also help to clarify my views.

Once upon a time there lived a small group of believers in a town. The people of that town became very hateful to the believers. The believers fled the town to save their lives. They felt tired and slept in a cave. When they awoke they felt hungry. They sent one man to bring food from the town they had left. When he entered the town, he was very cautious about his identity because if the people had recognized him, he would have been in danger. He produced the coins to buy food, but the shop keepers looked upon him very curiously and told him that the coins were very old and were not valid. The man walked through the town and saw that everything had changed. The whole generation had changed. He spoke to the people. The people had heard about those believers from their elders. They heard the whole story from the man and went with him to see the cave. They verified all the situations and the whole story and then they brought the believers to the town with much respect and agreed with them in their beliefs. For the men in the cave there had not passed one day, but for the people in the town many years had passed. Who was correct in the counting of time? Both sides were correct, but there was a difference in perception.

The God can make these differences in perception felt whenever and wherever He wants. He is almighty and the creator of time. People who die might perceive time very little as compared to those living.

Sleep is a rehearsal of death. Why sleep? If a man is fatigued he can lie down without sleep, but the God created sleep and sleep is necessary to rejuvenate the physical body. This is a sign from the God. How helpless a man is when he is asleep. He is unaware of the world and everything around him, and yet he enjoys sleeping. He consumes about half of his life in slumber. When he is sleeping, it does not matter for him whether he is rich or poor, mighty or weak, privileged or deprived. The God gets hold of him and then he is asleep, not conscious about the passing of time. He gets up and recalls in his mind all about himself, rich or poor, powerful or weak, relatives and friends, race and religion, time and date. After some moments he is what he was before he slept. Some people say time is money. Time can never be bought with money. Time is childhood, youth and old age. Can these be interchanged with money? Time is the God's creation and the God's creations have no alternatives. Time changes the powerful and powerless, rich and poor, happy and sad, many and few, honorable and disgraced and all whatever and whichever are in this universe.

Have you observed a person deeply involved and lost while watching a drama or film? Sometimes he is so engrossed in the story which begins from the childhood of a character and ends in his old age, that he forgets the actual perception of time. He thinks in the moments of his involvement that the time is really changing so fast. He takes some moments to bring himself back to the present. Here lies the difference in perception of time between living and dead. To the dead the lifetime can just seem a drama. Even for the elderly, their past time seems to them a drama. Time is a perception like eternity and cannot be subjected to just numerical counting.

THE GOD AND CEREMONIAL PRAYERS

Mankind has been praying to the one God or gods from the beginning of history and who knows how much before it was recorded. In the old times, there were nonsense, foolish and cruel ceremonies including sacrifices of human lives. All these ceremonial activities seemed to the concerned communities so sacred that they fought dreadful wars against each other. People, having different manners and methods of prayers, have been fighting against each other due to their disagreements. Some of these activities seem to the civilized world very absurd, but some likewise absurdities are continuing even now in today's modern world. Millions of people believe that these activities are much sacred and many are upholding these as customs and traditions of their forefathers.

The inclusion of Italian or Greek mythology in customs and traditions is understandable, but to take them as a belief is foolishness. Apart from these absurd activities, groups own their manners and methods and hold sacred those which they own. Those who dare to disagree are called apostates. So-called believers have to learn all these manners and methods, only then can they pray. While praying they should be very alert with regard to observance of these manners otherwise their prayers will be nullified. The praying persons keep their attention on the so called sacred manners and not on the God. The clergy tells them about the number of virtues they have earned by keeping these manners on numerical grounds.

The mystic poet Shah Hussain says, "Who is there intervening between lover and beloved, push him aside." (There should be no one between a sincere believer and the God. If there is, there may be no prayers and no true faith unless the believer feels direct interaction with the God.)

Different religions have different manners, days, time, languages and places to pray. All these differentiations are necessary to maintain their separate identities. The maintenance of these identities is their primary concern and for this very reason, the religions have separate names for every single one. Each religion has claims of superiority over every other one and this so-called superiority is a part of their beliefs. The God is not concerned with these identities and superiorities because these are not for the God, but only to satisfy their own self-righteousness. The God strongly dislikes all such thoughts and likes every manner and every word which is for Him only. To remember the God with sincerity, love, solemnity, fear and hope pleases the God no matter in which manner, language or place is used.

The mystic poet Bulleh Shah says,
"Mullah (Muslim clergy) pressed me hard to learn bay (second alphabet, next means prophet), but I only learnt alif (first alphabet), so he beat me and expelled me out." (All knowledge leads to one, the God, and no more is necessary.)

He says,
"Why I should go to Kabbah (the Muslim pilgrimage center)? My heart longs for Takhat Hazara (town of the local classical love story hero). People prostrate (their faces) towards Kabbah but I shall towards my beloved." (The God)

He says,
"The God is creator and master of all, does not matter you went to the Mosque and prayed after ablution, but without purification of heart you have merely stood like a column."

He says,
"Your (the God's) love has made me a non-believer (as people say) so a Muslim faith is not required."

If the founder of a religion (might be a prophet) gave his follower a particular day or days, weekly or yearly, this was to promote the sense of collectiveness, harmony and social celebrations. How can the God change one holy day with another and a holy place (the places already existing) with another? Is the God interested in architectural designs and splendor of the places of worship?

The mystic poet Sultan Bahoo says,
"The way to the God is not the prayers in mosques, keeping the fasts, leaving the affairs and attractions of the world and beauty (like a monk), but the way to the God is in good intentions of the heart and mind which the God knows."

The God prefers neither designs of prayer buildings nor the days or time of worship. He neither needs the meat of the sacrifices nor the hunger of the fasts if these do not evoke love and mercy. The same words uttered by different persons, in the same manner, in the same place have different weight and impact. This difference can be unimaginable. The God knows the best about intentions and sincerity. He can also measure the depth of the unspoken words which are not of any language. There isn't any time or place when and where the God should be prayed to, but most of the prayers of all religions are just ceremonies and not actually the prayers of the God.

He also says,
"Those who have found the way to one God need not the recitation of the Koran (Muslim holy book). They follow the way of love and thereby remove all the curtains." (Obstacles)

A CLERGY'S SERMON

Oh, my people, be happy, be merry, for you are the blessed born,
Your God has given you an upper hand over the rest of humanity,
Which he didn't give to any before the beginning of the religion you have,
And you still hold superiority over others, who agree not.

Be not worried if he sometimes puts you to trial and test,
You are the beloved of your God and for others he doesn't care,
Your God is supreme and he gave you the special name,
Those will face the curse by him who do not proclaim.

He likes your names and loves the landmarks you hold sacred,
He taught you how to build the places of worship and how to pray,
You are responsible to save the honors of your persons and books,
Be ready to respond with force and might if the others urge or dare.

Your forefathers did not fight the dreadful wars in vain,
To keep their message alive, you should be zealous in your belief,
I am sure your God will then reward you with the best place in paradise,
Which is forbidden to others, only to some will he allow the lowest phase?

If anyone says that the God is the God of mankind and the God of universe,
Don't heed, don't listen, he wants to grab the complacency you have,
Hold on strictly. Your God is happier when strict you are,
How can you and others be equal? Surely, he is the devil's disciple.

THE GOD AND MORALTIES

By name of God the Almighty, who created mankind of a nature most liked by Him? He is pleased when any human chooses the way to Him and remains constant despite all the inducements and temptations. He is the true and real guardian of mankind. He is omnipotent, omnipresent, doesn't sleep. He is benevolent and merciful. Being the Almighty, He over powers anger and pleasure. Being the Almighty, He neither feels elevated nor depressed.

He gave mankind most of his good qualities except those that only He is worthy of, so the morals are the same and will remain same in all civilizations. Some religions claim that they have superior rules and manners to follow because the God specially gave those to them. This is a false assumption. The God isn't and cannot be so unjust. How can He create such inequalities, being the creator of mankind and a true guardian? All the efforts and purposes are to have good social behaviors though rules can change from time to time and from region to region. Communities should demonstrate tolerance and forbearance. If they do not, their religion or the people who believe it are not true followers of the God.

Some societies impose restrictions upon individuals about the food they take, especially liquor. A person is human if he is in his senses. These senses make humans the superior creation. Anything should not be taken if it makes a person lose his senses. This act not only is harmful for the person, for society, it is much disliked by the God. Intoxication is harmful to one's body and is often illegal. Losing one's senses willingly, even as a result of anger, is harmful and not liked by the God. A person cannot pray and should not pray if he is not in his senses. Intoxication is not necessarily from liquor, but also drugs and feelings of superiority. Humans are free to take anything which is neat and clean and is not harmful for one's health.

The God doesn't want compulsion in faith, so society has no right to compel a person about when or not he can fast or eat. This is done in some communities in the name of holy days.

In the modern civilized world, people have better social behavior, but they do not necessarily have a better family life. In this respect, they have become selfish. As they enjoy the time of their youth, they forget their responsibilities towards their elders. They do not even give due time to their children. There isn't any harm in enjoying youth, but sometime that should be put aside for those who need attention. To deprive those in need of their due attention and affection is selfishness. Elders and seniors must be respected. Seniority in respect of age or relation should be acknowledged.

The God created males and females and created attraction and love among them. To make love is natural if both partners willingly do so, but humans are not animals, so some principles have to be followed in this relationship. There is love between sister and brother, daughter and father, mother and son, real uncle and real aunt, but even to discuss these relations as males and females will defile the purity of relations. Thank God all the civilizations have this sense of purity.

Rules and laws cannot be made for a better family life. There can be laws for duties but not for love or respect. No agreement or rule can make people or couples love each other. The government cannot issue orders to respect the elders but to provide justice and security to the people is government's duty. Human couples should not be only sex partners, but they should have the sense of deep and lasting relationship. Though the separation from each other is their right, this right should only be exercised after much consideration. Only a sense of lasting relationship can be the base of that love which is necessary for a better family life. All humans know that loyalty is a good quality. If one partner dislikes the other's disloyalty, he can separate himself. There has been much discussion on polygamy. Men often marry more than one woman and women do not marry more than one man. I think women can endure. if they do not like the polygamy of their partners, while men cannot. Moreover, if there are to be any offspring, polygamy of women is not practical. This matter should also be left as personal liberty and state law should not interfere in the matter.

The believers or the God's men surely have a loving nature, love for humanity and much love for their brothers, sisters, family elders, family friends, and family. Love is not exhausted by loving close relatives and friends, but the fact is if a person doesn't love near ones, he really cannot love anybody and cannot love humanity. A believer doesn't hate anybody except the cruel, unjust, selfish and evil. With love, humans can get rid of depression – without love, real happiness is impossible. Humanity very well knows social evils, and continuous struggles are required to control and decrease evils, though eradication is not possible.

THE PROTECTOR

God does not need anyone's help. He helps everyone who seeks His help who has a faith in Him as the only God. The God knows and controls the minutest movements in the universe. He gives life and keeps you living for a certain period. Nobody and no power can help you without His consent and approval. Nobody and no power can stop or hinder if He wants to help. It is by His consent that all communities, all races, all countries and the whole of humanity exist. It is by His consent that some rich and some are poor, some powerful and some are weak, some healthy and some are sick, some enjoy pleasure at one time and some at another time, some are sad at one time and others at another. Even than mostly people get proud and do not realize that everything is subject to change. Life itself is uncertain and temporary. Of course, happiness is the real goal to attain, but most humans do not know very well how to attain it.

The God protects you from severe cold, severe heat, saves you from thirst and hunger. A person who eats very simple food can be happier than the one who has all varieties available. A person who wears very simple clothing can be happier than the one who has costly costumes. A person living in a mud house can be happier than the one living in a majestic castle. If a man is shivering in severe cold…at that time he needs shelter and he doesn't long for a beautiful building. A hungry person needs food and doesn't require or wish for a delicious meal. A person in a state of severe danger prays for his own safety and does not plan to rule over others. When he is relieved of hunger, danger and has shelter, he expands the circle of his requirements. His wishes exceed the basic necessity. One can say there is no harm if these are within his reach, but most people make these extra necessities a part of their life and plunge into despair if they are not available. Humans are being tried by the God when he puts problems before them. The men of God pray for absolution and salvation and when they are relieved of that problem, they thank the God from the core of their hearts. The God likes this praying and thanking. The non-believers are desperate when they have problems and proud when they have none.

Are you boastful of having good health? And rule out the possibility of falling ill? Be thankful to the God if you are healthy and pray to the God for health if you are sick. Old age approaches when you will be as helpless as you were in your infancy. After all, there is a certain death. Are you boastful of your riches? Fear the God because there can be a situation even in this world when your riches cannot be of any use. Your riches can leave you indigent any time, so don't rely on them. Are you boastful of your friends and relatives? Don't you feel that there can be a situation when your friends cannot be of any help to you? Their feelings of friendship can also lessen or dissipate. None other can be so reliable. Are you feeling secure enough against any sudden catastrophe? Behold the very next moment your cherished security can be subverted and then all of you will say, "It is an accident." There cannot be a moment when your security is guaranteed. You are vulnerable from the beginning.

Pray and remember the God, only this will give you a sense of deep contentment and satisfaction and only He can save and protect you. He can create means for your protection beyond your imagination. Love the God as only He can give you the friendship that no other can. He makes your relatives and friends love you and He can change their love to hatred. Do not think it certain that you will be fed tomorrow or that you will enjoy health, festivity, company or life itself. Pray to the God and then be hopeful. Certainty and hope (however strong it may be) are different. Pray to the Protector for your protection, the protection of your dear ones, and the protection of all, especially those who are straightforward, kindhearted and loving.

THE MERCIFUL

Mankind does not take as blessings that which the God gives to all or many. The God made the earth. He makes rain fall and thereby grows crops and fruits. He made animals to serve us. We drink milk and eat meat. If these things are available to all, they are not appreciated by all and some will feel they are not the blessed. Had those been available to only a few, those receiving the bounty may be much happier. They feel difference and not actual reality. Men of the God pray to the merciful and beneficial God. Mankind does not even feel the reality of death because they see death of others and the world remains unchanged. The fact is, when a human dies, it doesn't matter to him if this universe remains or is eliminated. They are not grateful to the God for the sun, air and water because these are for all and not for special ones. So they do not worry about whether or not the earth takes in water of oceans to its inner core, and cycles of rains and snow stop. The moon also shines for all, so the blessings for humanity go unnoticed by individuals or groups.

Think about life a few centuries ago when humans did not have the facilities of present times… privileged people were happier and felt blessed. A common man of today has more luxuries of life than the privileged ones of old times yet he doesn't seem happier.

Almost all parents are very loving and merciful to their children, but children sometimes cannot understand some of the steps the parents take for their children's well being. Some measures taken by parents are well intended and well perceived, but children sometimes feel angry. For example, parents do not allow an infant to catch a burning piece of coal or allow a child to jump into a deep-water pool. Even then there is a possibility of parents being in the wrong, but the Almighty, The Omnipotent, the Merciful, is always just and right. Humans cannot perceive what He knows, as only He has the absolute knowledge. He is always merciful.

I have seen many ups and downs in my life including the death of my dear ones, which I would have averted at any possible cost if it were in my power. I have experienced many successes and failures and like everyone, I did not wish failures. In spite of all tragedies and failures, I am thankful to the God for his blessings upon me. He knows best and has been right and just. Without these tragedies and failures, I would have not gained maturity and insight, which by the grace of the God I now have. I believe he is surely the Merciful.

THE GOD AND CIVILIZATIONS

Humans are not certain about the time of their beginning or origin of life. They also don't know how they spread over lands on the whole world. The distances, fewer means of communication, different climates and different natural resources affected their lives in different ways resulting in different civilizations. These factors in any civilization are not objectionable, but many civilizations cherished and have been cherishing false beliefs against supremacy of the one, the God.

To pray to the God and ask for His favors is an inborn instinct in every human. This instinct is the basis of having a faith or belief. Self-righteous interpretations of this natural instinct made humanity divide into different religions. The instinct is the same, but claims of having better or best interpretations divided humanity. The God is one, but stress is laid upon personalities with claims of superiority of one or more over another. The God doesn't want humans to be engaged in such superfluous conflicts. The God sent his messengers not to establish their dignity, but to tell humanity about His supremacy and His supremacy alone. Whenever a prophet or true preacher challenged the false norms, customs and beliefs of any civilization, faced many difficulties. He/she was admonished not to interfere, otherwise to be ready to face dire consequences. The very thought of forsaking false beliefs of their forefathers fell heavily upon them and the so-called honorable people of society got very annoyed because they took it as a threat to their honor and power. In many civilizations people strayed and began praying to many gods and self-made idols. Their selfishness made them quarrel even regarding the supremacy of the idols. Every group claimed his idols and other belongings to be superior to the others'.

I think that many known religions of the world in the beginning were true and right. The followers were humble, cooperative and straight forward, but with the passage of time when they gained strength, they turned aggressive and proud with the intrusion of some or many misinterpretations. Their self-righteousness enticed them to claim that which they owned as superior, the only right and so-called truth. Their prayers lacked sincerity and changed into ceremonies which were an insult to the word, "PRAYERS."

In most cases the majority and power compelled people to change their religion, or prevailing socio-economic circumstances forced them to do so. In the beginning every true religion, when focus was only, "THE GOD," believers were very few. Most of them who joined the expansion trend were insincere claiming some basic advantages over the rest of humanity. Perhaps now these claims of special advantages is called fundamentalism?

Nature and forces of nature have nothing to do with any religion or belief, but people do consciously or unconsciously think that these are interconnected with their faith and civilizations. Land, trees, flowers, mountains, lakes, rivers, oceans, wind, clouds, birds, and animals have nothing to do with the faith of people living, although these do affect the lives of people, or become a part of their civilizations. The River Nile is neither Egyptian nor Arabic, neither Muslim nor any other religion, and the Himalayas or the Ganges have nothing to do with the Hindu religion. It doesn't matter to the water of the Ganges that the territory in which it flows is named India and people living on its bank hold this water sacred. Nature is not concerned with people but people are concerned with nature. Climates and weather don't bother about races or religions of people, but people do bother about, and have to bother about them.

The God, the creator of the universe and nature doesn't like or dislike races and civilizations. The God loves those who love Him, regardless of language, race or community. Nature is controlled by the God only and the God cares for His believers. Civilizations flourish or become extinct. They can remain constant for some time or change rapidly, but believers of the God have believed the same religion, the same basic ethics, and the same natural values whenever and wherever they live.

Love the God and do not have such love for anyone else. Only He is worthy of all praises, only He is center of all trusts and has the power to fulfill these all.

TO THE GOD

Oh, God, let me know to what community you belong,
And what community you prefer to be called as yours.

To what religion you have given the authority to be true,
And allowed to call all others heathen or damned?

With what rituals, and ceremonies you like to be pleased,
And to avoid your wrath, what must not be performed?

On your land where I have to pray and where not,
In what shapes of temples or what types of mosques?

What types of prayer leaders I have to follow,
Many claim that only they are aware of the right path.

Are you the God of divisions and not the God of all humans?
Not the God of the universe, but the God of pilgrimage lands?

Do you prefer one group of humans over all the rest?
And their ways or kinds of worship you hold the best?

THE GOD OF HUMANS

Mighty believers of mighty religions perform their majestic prayers in majestic buildings, struggling hard to outnumber and overpower each other. We are weak, but the God is Al-mighty, and it is not up to us to establish His supremacy, so we need not bother about it.

The mighty groups are knocking loudly at the doors of heaven, fierce contests are going on to subdue one another, and we are too weak to face their furious bravados, so we are standing aside, waiting patiently for our turn to be considered. You are the God of the universe and the God of humanity and we have faith in your mercy and benevolence. We do not reject their claims for being the first and only to enter your heaven, because it is upon you to decide, but they reject our hopes to be pardoned by you. Oh God of mankind, please help us.

I am an outlaw of so called religions.

My mystic poet says, "Is the religion brother of my wife (in an abusive sense) that I should care for? Do away with religion. It hampers the way to the God. Remove all obstacles between man and the God. Who is this, who intervenes between the lover and the beloved? Push him aside."

Groups are fighting with each other and I am fighting groups. I am sure I shall find friends and like-minded people. Free humanity and clear the way. No interventions are required between an individual human and the God.

Oh, the Beloved, reveal yourself to me. I heartily long for you.

Oh, my Lord, I pray to you in my heart, sometimes silently and sometimes in my words. Have I to learn special words and special language? My Lord, forgive me, if it is so, because it seems burdensome to me. I ask your favors very humbly, very sincerely and spontaneously as it comes to my mind, not observing the sacred manners or uttering sacred words; yet I hope you are equally mine as you can be to anyone else. No one else is my Lord, to no one else I shall bow and from no one else shall I beg, no matter if you accept me as yours or not.

I believe there are good humans all over the world who apparently have different religions, but actually they all seem to be the same. A meeting can be called to name their religions. If I am allowed to enter the names of some other existing religions, they can also be considered, but some are so hostile to each other that doing so would present quite a problem.

In the God we trust. Really?   Love your neighbors. Really?

DESTITUTE

Great is this world and so many great people in it,
Many have lived, many living and many will live,
Great by riches, great by powers and great by repute,
This greatness makes them not bother when they call us 'destitute.'

Proud to be great, proud to be rich and proud to be civilized,
They think that they are very just in keeping all they have,
Their civilizations teach that only they are just and we are wrong,
They don't like us to be among them and they keep away from the 'destitute.'

Great in power, great in might and great in numbers,
How can they be so generous to bear the dissenters?
They scorn, they disdain and they also see,
Some hidden dangers as they turn down the 'destitute.'

Great they might be, rich they might be and powerful they might be,
It is written in the history of mankind and the history of religions,
For so many times, the tables were turned over completely,
And one day, like it or not, they might be 'destitute.'

We live a simple life and can die a simple death,
Our Lord, the Lord of the universe, only your shelter we need,
We don't want powers, riches and much tasty feed,
We are satisfied with that which you give,
Give us peace to live. Are we 'destitute'?

THE GOD AND HUMAN WISHES

Humans are the supreme creation of the God but very few of them attain this level of superiority. With limited and uncertain life, humans try to change uncertainties into certainties according to their unlimited wishes and the God wants them to put their wishes under the God's will and be satisfied with what the God gives them. Because of their selfish wishes, they make desirable amendments and additions to a very simple belief that the God almighty is one - the God of mankind, the God of the universe, and they wrongfully attribute these wishful changes to the God. So, different religions are formed, religions based on what each likes or dislikes, and the various preference are inducted into such beliefs and faiths.

Claims of these preferences naturally divide humanity. Every group wants to promote its own religion, so there is a competition to overpower and excel over each other and as a result there are quarrels and fights often labeled holy wars. Every group in retaliation to other groups makes its desired changes so confrontations of desires and wishes take place in the name of the God. Fie on those who make their wishes their religion. Time passes on and such desired religions become the heritage of groups and nations. Every group feels proud of its heritage and traditional religion. Selfish wishers, selfish desirers and self-righteous religions want the God to favor their special preferences.

Human wishes have no end. A human being wishes to have good health and he never wants to lose good health, but his wishes cannot be confined in limits. He/she wishes to have a very long life that never ends. Wishes to be forever young…that old age never approaches. Wishes to be so strong that none can over-power and wishes to be so powerful that he can overturn mountains. Wishes to rule, to rule his family, nation, community, region, world and even the air, clouds and skies. Wishes to be aware of each and every-thing, to be aware of all happenings in the world and wants those happenings to occur as he/she wishes. He wishes to have the knowledge of all, what is going to happen and what has happened in the past that even history cannot cover. Wishes for self and for those whom loves unchallengeable safety in times to come, safety forever, leaving no chance for accidents or hazards.

He/she wants his superiority and the superiority what belongs to him/her, and wishes durability of this superiority to last forever. Wishes of humans also cover time after death when their physical being comes to an end, when they will no more feel sorrows, happiness, love and hate. This is an absurdity, but they wish that incidents and happenings would be as they wish even after their death as if they will be part of the living world. Suffering of many types are an essential part of human life. Selfish humans wish that if they are experiencing suffering others should also experience it or suffer more. This provides them with some consolation. If others have some sort of suffering which they do not have, it gives them a feeling of superiority, pride and much selfish satisfaction. A belief in the God keeps control and can overcome a human's selfish wishes.

The God wants humans to control these selfish and lofty wishes and desires; to be reasonable and rational in order to fulfill fundamental requirements for eligibility to believe in the God, and to fulfill the purpose of their supreme creation... Once a human becomes aware of such limitations and uncertainties of life, he is prone to despair. If in such a state of mind he seeks help and guidance from the Almighty, the Almighty very surely provides help, guidance, satisfaction and consolation to him and once he is a believer, he never feels hopelessness again.

Any selfish, cruel, wicked and proud person cannot be a believer. To wish is not a sin, but there are selfish as well as good wishes. If the wishes are good, and the help of the God Almighty is sought for fulfillment of these wishes, then the God is pleased because prayer is asking from the God. The God is almighty and there isn't any movement, happening or wish which isn't in his knowledge and power to comprehend. Good wishes and blessings for all mankind... "May the God show you and me the right path, guidance and belief." This is the best wish that one can ever wish.

A NOBLE'S WISH

I am a noble and among nobles I live,
Yes, I wish to supersede this noble's class,
I want much power and wish to be quite rich,
I am honorable and, I wish to be a brighter star.

My darling, you are Snow White with reddish cheeks,
I see stars twinkle when you smile and show your teeth,
You are beautiful; you are pretty from head to toe,
You are a rare beauty, the beauty which will never go.

Enjoy the supreme life in this lofty palace I have made,
Walk gallantly; be proud that I am yours and you are mine,
To mix with poor and common lowers your high place,
I picked you for me and you are now a noble's wife.

I wish I could get the endless life for you and me,
Forever I want to live and wish you never to die,
Cheer, cheer my love, I love your joyful style,
Be happy, only happy I want to be in all my life.

I wonder why in summer it rains on the Poor's house,
Why stars and moon shine there like on our place?
Why pretty birds sit there and also smell the spring air?
They also see the same beauty of nature and roam about everywhere.

Ah! Time has passed, years gone, she and I in this palace,
I wish a change in my love, but she doesn't know the fact,
Some poor build their homes upstream to make me much perplexed,
Some of them have pretty wives and they seem not too impressed.

Oh, my love, are you fed up and don't wish to live here anymore?
It seems you are concerned about and attached with common folk,
What? Their songs do charm you and you seem to be affected?
I perceive, you want to leave and to someone else you are attracted.

What do you say? I am selfish and that I am very proud?

Death might approach me, and I am growing old?
Oh no, oh my God! Why such nobles have to die?
What? The grave! No! I shall have a magnificent tomb.

THE GOD AND DEITIES

Mankind has been worshiping the God or its own deities from the beginning. Names of religions and ways of worship differ, but people have been asking favors from the invisible power or powers all over the world in all times. They used to perform various types of rituals for their satisfaction. Most of mankind inherited the rituals and ways of worship from their ancestors and often followed them very strictly. Many types of sacrifices were offered and to safeguard religions and rituals, armies fought furiously against each other. Warriors laid down their lives and killed others to please their concerned deities and to win many strong favors.

The God almighty, creator of the universe, hasn't any specific shape, body or dimension. He is invisible, has never been seen and will never be seen until the universe collapses or the existing world ends by His will. The God almighty is the creator of life and all the necessities of life. He is omnipotent and omnipresent. Many humans longed for and tried to make the God visible as they were not content with his invisibility. They felt it easy to believe in visible gods or deities more than an invisible God. This change continued with many alterations and many diversities from region to region and group to group. Feelings of inheritance from their forefathers and the passage of time has added much reverence to such beliefs and the basis of many strong religions was established. Messengers or believers of the God have been struggling to recall humanity towards one true belief, the belief which was and will remain unchanged from the very beginning of humanity until it ends.

You often see lovers who love the sight, belongings and all attributions of their beloved when the beloved is not present before them. This provides them a sort of consolation. Attributes of respected saints of different religions are held sacred and holy wars have been fought on the basis of such sacredness. Portraits and sculptures were made to embody the invisible or not physically present, so the gods and deities were fabricated so that those worshiped were present physically and visible. Self-righteousness caused one group to have its deities different from another's and to claim some sort of preference of the deity over another's. Each group claimed the sacredness of their own deities above the others.

The God almighty is the God of the universe, the God of mankind, so the instinct of grouping in self-righteous humans is not satisfied and they feel the tendency to have something special or superior. Such feelings of supremacy are causes of different religions spread all over the world, otherwise the religion of The God was and will remain the same from the beginning of mankind until it ends – the very simple belief that the God almighty is One with no essential additions.

Epics have been written relating to different myths that contain battles of deities, one group of deities fighting against the other. These deities had human-like emotions, suffering and pleasures so the stories seem interesting. These deities as characterized in the epics were wounded, suppressed, overwhelmed…they laughed and were pleased. Mortals' feelings were given to immortal deities. Such epics are interesting fairy tales intermixed with human-like wishes, sorrows and pleasures. Human idealism created some characters as heroes and were lovable. The God's universe is absolutely one unit and no deity interferes. He doesn't need anyone's help as He is the almighty, the sole creator of the universe and each and everything in it. He rules the universe very equitably without anyone's help or interference, by His will and not according to any individual or group's wishes.

THE GOD AND JUSTICE

Humanity has been practicing one form or another of justice from its beginning. Injustice was often done in the name of justice. Those who followed the rules very rarely acknowledged their mistakes...that injustice was taken for justice. Persons, nations, communities committed heinous inhuman cruelties and yet they said that justice was being done. Had they been put on the defensive as recipients the gravity of their injustices would have been revealed to them. Many times in history when the tables were turned, when the opposite side happened to gain power, the sense of justice was lost completely. During the bloody partition of the Indian sub-continent in 1947, both concerned parties did dreadful, in-human, horrible acts in the name of justice. Their religions allowed them, their religious leaders urged them, and their God or gods were not angry but apparently were pleased to see the looting, plundering, raping, burning of families and targeting of infants with spears before the eyes of their parents. Human history is full of such incidents, but no doubt some real and pure justice also existed among persons and nations, but it was rare. The causes of such so called justice were no doubt abhorred by some; but self-righteousness with regard to their respective caste, race, nation, religion and wealth drove many. Desires to have and gain supremacy over others who do not share their beliefs and the desire to gain more power and safety justified their atrocities.

Human civilization has progressed positively towards gaining insight into the behavior of humans and human rights. I have some personal reservations about harm done to natural family life, irrespective of religion or religions. The God created humans, but most humans are infected with selfish desires and very few are able to preserve the God-given humanism. Believers of the God surely have insight into humanism and justice, totally unbiased justice, and those who have not the capability are so called self-declared believers.

Some religions or regional communal groups have been practicing, and some still desire to practice blind cruel justice which spreads hatred, depression and anger. Such justice is suppressive in its nature, so victims develop a desire to resist and revolt, if possible, against law, or religion itself. As a result, civilized communities don't want such laws to be practiced although books containing such laws are held sacred by them. This is a disparity, but followers won't bother with and don't wish to ponder such matters.

The requirement of justice differs from case to case. Each individual case or person concerned requires a separate approach for proper judgment. Criteria and purpose of such judgment should be a promotion of love and peace among humans and not merely punishment. If love and peace are in danger then the appropriate punishment must be awarded, light or harsh according to the nature of the crime and atrocity committed. Justice with love is approved if it works, especially when the offender or offenders have lost the power of aggression and acknowledge the crime. Liberty and equality among persons, communities, and groups is the necessary factor of justice and personal freedom, as long as it is assured that it will not harm others.

The various claims of power over others are harmful for social justice.
Let love rule. If its rule is threatened, justice should intervene with required force and might. To struggle or to provide force for justice is Godly.

DEFEATED AND VICTORIOUS

I am a ruler with my glittering badges and shining ropes,
I love to rule, not to be ruled. To rule is the real life,
Those should be ruled by whom the God has chosen to rule,
For betterment of the people and to keep the world running smoothly.

How can ordinary people understand the art of ruling?
This is the God that doesn't want them to be powerful or rich,
These delicacies can never be entrusted to the people of lower minds,
If by chance it happens they feel proud…I know that pride is a crime.

I have always been victorious and victory I love,
To hold down the rising ups is for me just fun,
So wisely I see through that I know, events to come,
Such dignity and glory I have, yet I am not a proud one.

I was defeated once, but I don't want to remember that,
I envied a simple man while hidden in the wilderness,
He went to the city forbidden to me and he was careless,
I searched for and kicked him out when I was not powerless.

I prayed to the God, the Almighty and defeated I was,
That I shall be merciful and forever serve just cause,
Much depressed I felt as I had lost my dear ones,
O God! I shall not take revenge if I ever overcome.

My friends said, "It is very just in wars to disgrace and kill,
Mercy will never work…do much more than they did."
Then they skillfully hunted women, children, young and old,
My learned clergies made me believe that my power is the God's will.

So I built for people, for clergies magnificent buildings in which to pray,
I think the God is much pleased when worshiped in a full and dignified way,
Down with enemies of our faith, blessings for the sacred throne,
The God will never favor enemies, with much surety as they say.

LIFE AND DEATH

We don't know how precious life is and we don't have a scale to measure it. If we asked a young poor boy if it were possible to change his life with a very rich elder person, would he agree to it? He may not agree at all if he has a sense of life. Any material gain can't be a substitute for life. A person's life is the whole of mankind by itself. A person dies and leaves behind all the relations and affiliations contracted during lifetime. After death a person has not any race, language, caste, cult, motherland or anything that deemed his/her own. Alas, not many persons realize this. They think they will be a part of all those, and will observe and enjoy all the hatreds, loves, vengeance, likes and dislikes when as were alive. If a person could realize death in its absolute real sense, it could be easy to understand the purpose of life. But, no matter how precious life may be, we all have to die sooner or later. Everything must end except the God. Life is too short to be gratified even if it were doubled, tripled or....

Shall we perish totally? No, I don't believe this. This is too horrible to think; and the God has not created me to end like this. The God has sparked in me a soul which desires to live an endless life and will not be content with less.

No matter if death comes, we should not put our lives in jeopardy without a cause. Life has no alternative. But when there is a just cause, life may be sacrificed, and this is Godly. The God has given life and it should only be given in the name of the God. All noble causes and actions are liked by the God. Protecting the innocent, including oneself, helping the needy, or fulfilling moral obligations are Godly actions. We must perform those in the name of God.

If a person dies a sudden death or any kind of a natural death and is a believer, has also given his life to God. To take the life of any person without a just cause is a very big sin. It should never be taken with evil intent. Again, it is necessary to take life in the name of the God. A fight for justice is Godly. Love mankind, and above all, love the God. Except the God, everyone is vulnerable to evil. To do well is Godly and the God is with every good deed.

I have to say that humans are born and humans die. When a baby is born he recognizes his mother when she feeds with her breast and gives a mother's love. Then baby becomes aware of his/her surroundings, people, relations, friends, enemies, religions, forefathers, and the history of forefathers, nations and races. He/she is a human. We tell him/her and teach about all these attachments. These attachments are neither good nor bad, but when humans grow selfish and proud on the basis of these attachments, it is bad and un-Godly. Humans should try to suppress such feelings. Total suppression of such feelings is not impossible, but is very difficult. The God loves those who strive to suppress un-Godly feelings. By this I mean, humans are born neither Christian nor Muslims, neither Europeans nor Asians, neither good nor bad.

When a person dies, it is again the death of a human, neither rich nor poor, neither noble nor mean, neither honorable nor disgraced, neither Israelite nor Palestinian, neither Indian nor Pakistani, but a human only. Our efforts to decide how great their lives have been cannot make any difference to dead humans, no matter how big the disparity might seem to those who are living, looking and feeling. Different ceremonies, big ceremonies, small ceremonies, no ceremonies cannot make any difference at all to the deceased, but only to satisfy those left to mourn or claim to be attached to him/her. I do not mean that on their part this is not good. This is natural to feel the separation of those who are beloved, dear and in the larger context, good humans. These feelings can be the base of prayers for the departed soul. This is good and not at all bad. I shall desire a prayer by good, sincere friends rather than those who hold high offices in any community, cherish high esteem and repute, even if they pray in the most holy places, because their prayers for me will be ceremonial, and from good friends I expect sincerity. Sincerity can also be expected from unknown good humans.

Any human who dies leaves behind all the attachments contracted in this world. His/her dead body should be respected by all, even by enemies if they have killed, because that was a human; not their enemy. Their enemy died and is no more. To be buried or burned makes no difference to dead, although I think to bury is better. In the God I trust and I pray to make this the basis of my satisfaction forever.

LIBERALISM VERSUS FUNDAMENTALISM

Is liberalism good and fundamentalism bad? Many would say, "Yes!" But many in this world say, "No." The religion of those who say no demands this fundamentalism. How can one be liberal about commands from the God? Do commands from God need modification and changing? Does God need to be civilized? Certainly, there aren't any answers to such questions. If religions are practiced according to the fundamentalists, they will engulf the world in chaos leaving no room for peace and harmony. The God's command may be or perhaps is, "Ask them to change their religions. If they don't accept, you have authority to rule over them by force and take them under your power." What is right and what wrong? Might and diplomacy will decide. Certainly, the God is almighty and the only supreme. Peaceful co-existence and mutual respect is liberalism, but what about the commands from God?

The civilized world has framed some human rights that their concerned religions and clergies have been denying them. It seems that they have made good progress, but the question still is, does the God's principal change, or can his commands be modernized? If so, I shall not have such a God and perhaps many others think as I do. Most people do not think deeply about the God and are merely followers of their inherited religion and maybe hardliners, and those who do not take religion seriously are also called liberals. I believe the God whose commands and principals will never be changed. Manmade human rights which can be modified for betterment, but rights granted to humans by the God are forever supreme and freedom of thought is one of them.

My friends, if you will allow me, I want to define liberalism in my own words. No doubt liberalism is freedom of thought. I hope you will not mind and let me say that whosoever claims to be a follower of his respective religion without this freedom of thought is a fanatic, a so-called believer of the God; and those who deny and want to deny this freedom to others are anti-God. Actual liberalism demands from humans to let others say what they want to say, listen passively to all thoughts and views, ponder them cool-mindedly and then say yes or no. Obstinacy is the greatest ignorance and the God hates it. You may be right, but don't reject others outright. This is obstinacy and fundamentalism. Be prepared to accept more truth if you come across it. If you shut the door to your mind and heart, you are not confident, and you fear to lose something. Better to lose than to have something false. Wisdom is a most essential part of true belief and a wise person is never proud of anything including knowledge and he keeps searching for knowledge until his death. Liberalism means others may be in the right; so, think about it and if you are not willing to think, you may be a so-called believer, or not a believer at all.

Liberalism is to see one's self in daylight; he/she may be good, less good, or not good at all. Fundamentalists don't dare to come into the light. They keep on insisting that they are good, or best without any exposure to the light. They conceal reality.

Liberals say, "We may be wrong." Fundamentalists would not say such words, or they might be called liberals, because fundamentalists have always to be right.

Allow all humanity to choose its own way. Only then may people be real believers or not. Don't try to keep them away from daylight; neither believers, nor non-believers.

I wish for all – tolerance, forbearance, freedom of thought in its real sense for each and everyone because there can't be any belief without it. The unwise can never find the God and any formal or religious education isn't necessary for wisdom.

May the God bless all of you.

THE CHANGING WORLD

The world has changed much and we all are aware of the degree of change. We have been told about the Stone Age and similar primitive societies, but we are not quite positive about the times and histories of these changes. We have dug from the earth evidence of some well-established civilizations. How or when they perished, we do not know exactly. One thing we do know is that they had their organized systems of life and society. Even in recent times there have been humans in some parts of the world who wear no clothes, have no permanent homes, villages or towns. They live the most primitive life that humans can live.

As we know, humans have been progressing in building new settlements, villages, towns, and cities. The building of boats and transporting across water was an ancient art, but according to the history we know, it is modern civilization that sailed across oceans, making discoveries of new lands and eventually every inch of our world has been explored. We don't know at all how mankind spread over all these vast lands so far from each other. The civilized world has also explored undeveloped and underdeveloped regions and societies of the world, governed them and sooner or later they won or were granted their freedom. The ruling civilizations no doubt left them more orderly, more educated, and more civilized than they were before. Many such nations and people also adopted the religions of the governing nations. In many cases the religions they had before were eccentric, unrealistic, so the changes were comparatively better. Even now-a-days generally unrealistic religions are losing ground. Most people continue to follow the old religions as traditions and customs of their land and forefathers because they don't like to part with them.

Mankind had never such freedom before as it has now although individual freedom to humans is not yet granted or it is only partially granted in many parts of the world. No doubt we humans have made great progress with-regard to society, civilization, life, freedom, mutual understanding, and, you may say in the field of religion also. Life seems to be safer, more settled and easy, especially in developed countries. In underdeveloped countries, it is still very hard. There have been tremendous successes in all sorts of technology making life much easier. Humans in advanced countries don't want to imagine life without these improvements. Modern means of communication and telecommunication have brought people much closer the world over.

The world never experienced such settled boundaries a century or two ago. There weren't any passports and people could move into different regions without any documents. Nearly a century ago, there wasn't any notion of overpopulation. There were many uncultivated lands lying in different regions. There weren't any endangered species of birds or animals. Sources of land and water were thought to be unlimited. No weapons of mass destruction were invented and no harm to nature or environments noticeable. It is with the help of modern science and technology that we know that natural sources are measurable and could be endangered. Life continues almost on the same pattern as it had been hundreds, thousands of years or more ago…before the advent of modern civilization. Scientists are trying to explore the very beginning of human life and life itself.

People of this modern world are making efforts to make life safer than ever before. They don't want to go through any horrible events which could harm their settled and peaceful lives. They do think their prosperity will grow. This is a genuine human wish; therefore, it need not be criticized. Rivals of the past are now friends and allies. The wish for peace among humans is increasing. This is also a good sign. Mankind had never peace-keeping bodies or any peace awards. Efforts are being made for a settled world order and to overcome uncertainties, which seem to be much greater than in the past.

Why have such changes happened to be in the more recent years or centuries? Why didn't mankind progress so quickly many centuries ago? Is this by chance, or were people in the old ages not so intelligent? If this is by chance, does the God want this world of ours to reach a culmination point? Humans have been striving for all kinds of certainties pertaining to their lives; but many times, progress has brought great disasters such as we witness in all the wars of the world. Changes are inevitable and natural. Certainties can never be taken for granted. The world is heading towards changes or maybe even one BIG change. Are you ready? When are these changes going to happen, and what will be the nature of such changes? Only the God knows. Many religions call this time of change, "The Day of Judgment." For believers of the God, such changes may not be astounding, but for others, they will be. Believe in the God, for only He can bless you with that satisfaction you require, not your self-created certainties. Self-protection and striving for a better life and atmosphere is human.

THE NECESSITIES OF HUMAN LIFE

Humans have always lived their lives in different situations and circumstances. Health, riches, power, honor are considered positive, while sickness, poverty, weakness and disgrace are taken as negative aspects of life. Besides these positive aspects, there are some other aspects which bring happiness to life. Happiness is the real motive to achieve. It may be with all, some, or none of these no doubt very important aspects. Other than spiritual and non-physical aspects of love and peace, there are inseparable physical aspects.

Humans cannot be happy in extreme hunger, thirst, pain, sickness or suppression. One has to be relieved of all such sufferings before others can expect normal behavior from him/her. Only then can anyone talk to him of spirituality or love. If anybody knows that his fellow human is suffering and does nothing to relieve the other from these sufferings, doesn't have any sort of spirituality. To help others is very Godly. Wouldn't you think that to have three or four pieces of bread and not offer one to an extremely hungry person, is inhuman? To have any inclination towards spirituality is good. If anyone has any awareness of spirituality, the God wants him to call on others to share it with him. It becomes necessary. When a human isn't under pressure of suffering, there comes another physical necessity of human life and that is having a sex partner. This desire is also a God-given desire, so it is natural and need not be suppressed. Some rules and ethics have to be observed because humans live socially. They are the supreme creation of the God and are not animals. It is observed that sometimes this desire of humans becomes abnormal and crosses the limits of decency which harms the ethics of a civilized society and, also the possibility of spirituality in those humans. To live a normal life doesn't mean suppression of this natural desire and necessity. Extreme selfishness in any aspect of life is harmful.

The world is now developing as a global village and it becomes binding upon all humanity to strive for availability of these necessities of life for those who are without. Good humans are kind to their families, neighborhoods, localities, nations and, also humanity in general. There is a natural level of fulfilling these basic-necessities. A person in acute hunger requires food and not a costly meal, and a person dying of thirst does not desire a branded soft drink, but only simple water. Similarly, a person in extreme hot or cold needs and wishes for a shelter - not a fine majestic building. Those who have ever experienced such situations know very well what they desired at the time, if not now when they are not facing the calamities. If some humans have these basic-necessities, they may be happier than those who have much in addition to the basic necessities. Even good health cannot be purchased. Other sufferings are not necessarily avoidable simply by the availability of better sources.

We can't define perfectly what honor is. In some parts of the world, it is a mixture of power, riches and majority. Honor itself is not a bad thing and it isn't a basic necessity of human life, but those who have it sometimes try to make the lives of those who haven't miserable. To be proud of it and misuse it against those who have not, is bad. Some who have been "honored" want to be reminded continually that they "have" and others "haven't"; otherwise, their honor would mean nothing. With the help of their so-called honor, they are often suppressors and aggressors. Not honor per se, but to remain safe from terror and suppression of those who have it, can be called a necessity of human life. The God's humans win love from their humanity and not necessarily any so-called honor. This is all they ask.

Then there are spiritual necessities such as the necessity of love, love of children, families, friends, community, humanity and the God. For example, ask a mother the value of her baby. She may not be ready to part with her child for all the wealth in the world, so the spiritual necessity cannot be measured in material gains. There can be such love in other human relations, so love and sacrifice for others are the spiritual aspects of human life. If this aspect of human life is not satisfactory, there can't be any real happiness. This is an appetite of the soul and must not be quenched. Sometimes starvation for love makes life worse. Persons not having any sort of love in their lives are actually emotionally destitute. Humans in love with each other in all their relations are really happy and those who love the God make their love on more solid grounds. They gain a depth of satisfaction which only they can have. Those who don't love humanity cannot love the God and are not the God's humans.

FREEDOM

What is freedom? It is not easy, at least for me, to define properly. All I know is that it is very lovely, very enchanting, and blessed are those who really enjoy it. Many are only labeled with it. Humans are born free, but alas, many become slaves to traditions, religions, false social ethics, power and majority. To enslave humans is certainly inhuman and, as I believe, is also un-Godly.

Freedom is largely known as the freedom of nations. Many nations fought for it from colonial powers and they celebrate their success throughout the world. Grand ceremonies are performed as the nations are proud to have won their freedom. Many countries made great sacrifices of human lives to get their liberty, but in several cases this was not actual freedom, but just a so-called freedom. This doesn't mean that there was more liberty under foreign rule, but it could have been. Perhaps there is a one recent example of a tiny Chinese territory gaining their liberty from a foreign rule. Liberty may be taken in the name of freedom but sometimes humans like to be governed by those who are from their own race, language, and beliefs. If North Korea took over South Korea, will they say that they have won freedom for their fellows? Would they be justified in their claim?

If I had to define freedom, I would say that freedom is basically a personal and human matter. If an individual's independence is not at stake, only then collective or national freedom matters. Slavery means slavery and it doesn't matter much who the master is. However, a beneficial, kind-hearted person who allows some or more freedom is no doubt a better master...it doesn't matter whether belongs to a particular nation. Suppression is punishment and its effects are not mitigated if perpetrated by one's own community or nation. If a human hasn't genuine personal freedom, so-called national freedom hasn't any charm for him either.

Some nations having won their freedom are enjoying it as a nation, but in many parts of the world only concerned armies, bureaucrats and influential persons enjoy the autonomy. Generals and other so-called leaders are continuously deceiving their public that national freedoms are great achievements, so they keep on celebrating with enthusiasm. False enthusiasm based on ignorance detracts attention from real problems as well as actual independence. Many-times this enthusiasm encourages personal sacrifice of lives. This enthusiasm can also be used to suppress opposite views declaring them as anti-national. Freedom under military rule, freedom under despots, needs to be outlawed, but very often even intolerant majorities prove very suppressive to an individual's freedom. If anybody remains a part of this majority may be at peace, but if anyone is sensitive enough to think of his own personal freedom, then there is a serious problem. I believe only such persons may be believers of the God and others as a whole may not be. Only a free mind (may not be physically free) can find the God and not a mental slave.

A free vision begets a real belief. With the help of this vision humans decide what to believe, to believe or not, to follow or not, to do or not, to say yes or no. They are able to choose or have an independent view, their own view. This vision is prohibited for none, but very few bother about it and keep on having others' beliefs, not their own. You could say that they have a disciplined belief. I think the God prefers those who come to Him by their own free will, a will of their choice and not a disciplined will, a majority's will, a forced will and, also a will of traditions or forefathers.

Those who are in search of freedom can't shout on the streets, "We want freedom, we want freedom." Because they are already free, action would be dealt with severely by the public or authorities. There are regional and international forums for nations to discus or redress their grievances; but for individuals who are victims of unjust suppression, there isn't any effective body. We can hope that someday mankind will make sufficient progress and all humans will have true freedom.

THE QUEST FOR PEACE

In human history, valiant warriors have won great reputations. They were and still are held in great esteem by their respective nations. Many of them made conquests to enslave other nations and to expand their rule. Too many were slain by armies of great generals of the past like Alexander, Genghis Khan and Tamerlane, but their respective nations haven't seen many benefits of their conquests. Does only fame or lust for expeditions justify killings of innumerable humans, horrors and hardships? However, those who fought to defend their people from the atrocities of conquerors and robbers were the real heroes. Many-times wars were fought in the name of religion and, I believe, not for the God, except those which were fought to liberate people from oppression, tyranny, or to provide protection for the weak. The world wars were too horrible, but war-waging nations sustained greater losses for no aims or real purpose. All these wars brought misery to the common men who were be-fooled by their leaders.

Mankind is divided into many groups: religious, racial, language… Horrible wars were fought on basis of such divisions and warriors' lust for power, the wish to rule others and to live a life of so-called excellence. This caused serious suffering and calamity for humans the world over. Religions (even before today's main religions) had divided humans more deeply than any other factor. Heinous crimes have been committed in the name of the God. The modern civilized world is also paying for so-called sacred causes. This has been and perhaps is a most serious threat because the God wants them to supersede others to bring them under their rule and join them in their faith. Self-righteous wishes for racial supremacy also brought huge misery to the world. Apart from these divisions, powerful and influential people or groups within communities have often suppressed humans unjustly and cruelly.

Peace is soft, lovely and dreamful as cool air is for a sun-stricken lonely traveler in hot summers, or one who finds a warm cottage when stranded in a frozen region. Those who don't wish for peace are inhuman and if their religion or any other ideology demands them to be otherwise are hateful. To have or achieve the power to defend peace is just, but those who use it to destroy peace are detestable. Many believe that peace is good, but don't know how to achieve and maintain it. The answer is not easy and involves many complications.

I believe that hardliners, harsh speaking people do not love and so are not loveable. They are conceited and proud. Pride of any sort is itself against peace and can at any time cause conflict, especially when confronted with any other pride. Stubborn people are not liked by gentle and polite humans. Stubborn people often create a nuisance in society and nations and cause disruptions wherever they live. They are rough and so hurt the softness of peace.

Many believe that humans have equal rights, but not many understand that the God is the God of mankind and not only their God. Why do they bother if anyone speaks against the God? This is a matter between that person and the God. If humans do not quarrel for speaking against the God, then quarreling on other matters is unnecessary. While the God only is most sacred, all other religious matters are of secondary importance. Still in many regions and countries, or with so-called democracies, only persons with a particular faith are allowed free demonstrations according to their faith and are eligible to hold high offices, denying others their genuine rights. If anybody believes the God, how can he consider himself superior by race? The God created all humans equal and nobody was born in a race by his own choice, but by the will of the God.

To live and let live can be a perfect base for a sustainable, lasting peace, but quarrelsome people often make different explanations to justify their self-righteous designs. Democracy is no doubt the best form of government with some human lapses, but in many countries is not practiced in its true spirit, or not practiced at all. Personal freedom, you may say, basic human rights are only partially granted or not granted at all. Only ignorant people can live with some ease under suppression. Ignorance itself cannot be reliable and is dangerous.

Suppression breeds hatred. Hatred can be the cause of conflicts. So, if ignorance and suppression exist, peace will remain at stake. War and peace are opposite to each other, but war against ignorance and suppression has to be fought for the cause of peace. Governments have their strategic and diplomatic policies and will not be willing to declare such a war openly, but such a war is only a matter of time. Go for it irrespective of religion, race or any other division and provide the world with the stability it needs. If you can provide humans their due freedom and rights, they will surely be helpful in maintaining peace in the world which is now called a global village. Beside this, every human has his basic needs of food, shelter and some other requirements. How can they wish for peace if these are not provided? Obey the God and then pray for peace. Peace is good and unjust bloodshed is very bad. So, a wish for peace is Godly and to make efforts for it, very Godly.

TO BE A HUMAN

It is noticed that people have been claiming their affiliations on various grounds. Many claim that their first close connection is on religious grounds, others claim on racial or national grounds. Of-course there are second and third preferences too. Perhaps very few will say that first of all they are humans. This term is not understandable to many because people like to have associations which differentiate them from others. They would not want one which provides preference over none other.

My mystic poet says, "Away with enmity, the Muslim nobles and Hindus are not apart; the God resides in all or possess all."

He didn't mean only these two groups, but he had in his mind a wider range and scope which covers all groups of humans in all regions. I am sure he didn't have any affiliation or preference in his mind – only that of a human. I believe that whenever there happens to be a savior or redeemer of mankind, demands call or teachings to be considered on humanitarian, secular grounds and wants opponents to free and relieve humans to adopt their own way by their own free will. Mighty opponents insist on keeping common people under suppression to avoid any risk of settled or established orders. Besides this, the weak in every part of the world in all times have been demanding from the powerful to be human; but alas if they in turn happen to become powerful after some time. They probably would not concede to be humans, but instead choose ethical, racial or another differentiation.

As I have already mentioned in my writings, in my opinion any formal or religious education isn't necessary for wisdom. Suppose a human happened to live with his small group of people in a remote tiny island, and was not aware of any outside world. That person could be as wise as persons living in a civilized or developed world. Then, which community or race would you ask him to join?

The mystic poets I have been referring to knew nothing about any philosophy and did not care about any certified teachings. They were actually free humans.

"Friend, say no for any more knowledge, only one alif (first alphabet, the God) you require." He often condemns knowledge of a clergy and says, "His knowledge has confounded him and he is bewildered."

Free humans also have their traditions or customs. For example, the mystic poet usually gives expression to his feelings with the help of a local love story of the Punjab (such as Romeo and Juliet), in which clergies wished to ban reading as anti-religious or vulgar.

"Continuously calling the name of Ranjha (hero), I am so involved that there isn't left Heer (heroin) any more". I enjoy an ecstasy and up-lifting when I listen or read such poetry. Such ecstasy can't be felt through an alien language, especially when it is not easily understandable. But for the clergy, this is heresy I believe that prayers can be said without observing any ceremony as passionate love and heart-felt feelings will break away any bindings.

Here is an example (just to explain).
Once upon a time; an intellectual believer of the God was passing by a wood. He heard a voice and stopped to listen. A shepherd was saying, "Oh, my God, if I happened to find you, I would comb your hair, fetch the best things from the wood and give air to my flute as long as it would please you." The believer went to the shepherd and admonished him not to speak like that because the God doesn't need all that and the God wouldn't be present before him physically anyway. The shepherd was quite disappointed.

When the believer was sleeping that night, he saw in his dream that the God was angry with him for having chastised one of his lovers. Early the next morning the believer again went to the same spot and waited for the shepherd to come. When the shepherd came, he asked him for forgiveness and told him that the God wanted him to keep on praying whatever way he liked. The shepherd replied, "I was also aware of that fact, but I was under an instant wave of emotions and you did indeed break my heart."

Love humanity, love the God and if you love your traditions, customs and homeland, don't hate others'. Bigotry of all sorts isn't good. I believe that a true believer of the God does possess the ability and has the insight to change his first affiliation to that of a human.

MAJORITY VS MINORITY

In almost every field majority is considered strength so religions also strived and still strive to gain greatness in everything. Such efforts aren't bad and people should be at liberty to convince each other, but very often importance is gained by power and not by convincing or preaching. Is multitude itself a blessing? I doubt it because in my view quantity has some drawbacks. No doubt to be a member of an important community is considered better, safer and privileged.

Every community in its beginning consisted of a few members. I think those members were very often in the right and, also were very sincere. They were not at all aggressive and attracted others by their superior morals and rightful causes. They had strong attachments with each other and shared troubles, suffering and other matters. Even today whichever community happens to be in the minority in any region, its members are close to each other and have more solid links than one in the majority. The fewer the membership is of a community, the closer they are in their relations.

Religions have often gained greatness by conquests or power, and it continued by being passed down through the ages. Their respective beliefs, not being questioned or debated openly, became stagnant and lost the fragrance of freshness. Often these majorities were divided on various issues. Because they were not truly sincere with their beliefs, many dreadful battles were fought within such communities on political and other grounds. Fighting groups killed humans who had the same beliefs on both sides!

Some large groups abiding by their religious laws will not allow their followers any option for a change of religion. Because any such change would mean a death sentence, perhaps they don't want anyone to lose God's heaven once it is ascertained. A change of religion in hardliner communities will also bring enormous social hardships, unbearable for an individual. However, minorities are at liberty to make changes. The powerful also don't want anyone to abandon their religion and then join another.

I believe that the God cares for an individual if he is a sincere believer. He may not care for a big majority, so multiplicity in religion isn't as good as in a democracy and may not be good at all. Had the God wanted it, there would have been only believers, but He likes his humans to be faithful to Him not by compulsion or might, but by their own free will. Have you heard about the king who disguised himself to know the real feelings of his people, relatives and nobles about him? We all would wish to know such feelings if it were possible.

A few sincere friends are far better than a many having only a transitory relationship. If put to a test, they may not only leave, but could also prove hostile. The God likes actual sincere believers and not multitudes consisting of traditional, hereditary, compulsory or socially economically bound believers. Majority or large gatherings for prayers doesn't mean more or easier acceptance by the God. Such prayers are mostly only ceremonial and void of sincerity. The communication revolution is bridging the gap between majorities, minorities or other ethical groups. It is hoped that one day such divisions will not remain deeply rooted and humans will be at liberty to search and find out the truth from wherever they like to get it.

YOU MAY BE RIGHT

You may be right and, I am not hostile to you,
I may be wrong, allow me some time to go through,
You have the divine and divinity, so not challengeable,
I shall obey also but let me see, if I am eligible.

You will serve your divine if you don't allow me to dissent,
You will do your job of any possible mischief to prevent,
But, will he accept me even if my heart is not prepared?
Yes, he will certainly do so, if of this he is not aware.

I know you can use physical and, also social suppression,
This will certainly make me agree with your suggestion,
I swear if you bear me as whatever I believe,
I shall never, but not mind if you speak against my belief.

If you will pray loudly, I shall do without a voice,
Never interrupt in your worships and shall not make any noise,
My God, the God of all doesn't want me to clash for His honor,
So, please don't shut me out, though it is in your power.

IN THE NAME OF GOD

In the name of God, the most beneficent and the most merciful, mankind has been performing many deeds including sacrifices of human lives. Massacres, subjugations, heinous cruelties against opponents were also perpetrated for the sake of God. If there is only one God why then is there oppression and suppression of opposing groups to please the God, or in the name of God? Is He the God of killers and the killed, suppressors and the suppressed, the mighty and the weak, the cruel and the loving, allies and hostiles? If so, then there are so many uncertainties. Just who are entitled or privileged to act or perform in the name of God.

Sacrifices have been made and holy deeds have been performed in the name of God though very rarely. The God does not share his name with anyone else or with any other purpose and motive. For the sake of God, in the name of God is to be only for the sake of God, in the name of God and not for the sake of religions, communities, groups or any other motives. People mostly pray because their religion demands it, not actually for the God's sake. Is construction of beautiful magnificent places of worship for the sake of God? No, this is for the sake of religion, a willing architect, their pride and ostentation. Most people help others financially as their religious, communal and moral obligation or to enhance their reputation. This is socially good, but not in the name of God. People mostly fight for their individual or collective motives which include religious motives and not for the God's sake. People even willingly die for religions or nations and not actually in the name of God. It may be absurd, but they also think of a respect or good reputation after death. What does this respect or reputation mean for them when they will never be present to feel or enjoy it? What sense do they make of it? This seems to me very strange or insensible.

Good deeds are Godly and bad deeds are un-Godly, so bad deeds cannot be done in the name of God. If good deeds are done for reputation or for any other motive including that of gratitude from a beneficiary, they cannot be for the God's sake. The sacrifice of a dry piece of bread by a hungry man who has not much bread with him to satisfy his own hunger, for another hungry person can be of great worth to the God; more than the sacrifice of a large food store by a wealthy person though everyone should sacrifice according to his capability or situation. To bear a minor injury in the name of God is of more worth than a hundred thousand lives lost for other motives. Life or lives must be sacrificed when the situation is such because life is a blessing entrusted upon humans by the God. To pray to the God is highly befitting of humans because it depends upon sincerity and depth of feelings of concerned persons if prayed for the sake of God and in the name of God. People have been interpreting their wishes, prejudices, likings and desires as in the name of God very selfishly. Crucifixion of Christ, mass killing of Jews, butchering by swords, stoning to death, whipping by lashes, disgracing humans in the name of God, is actually in the name of religion. Teaching codes and rules of prayers by clergies, keeping fasts and pilgrimages are mostly performed in the name of religion and not at all in the name of God and not at all entirely exclusively in the name of God.

"Oh God, are you being prayed to in worship sights and holy places banned for out-siders entry? Are your places desecrated by people who don't possess certificates issued by authorities? Have you appointed them over us? If so, why are there so many opposing each other? To which authority should we be submissive? If we know that any such authority has your approval, we should not only obey and respect them, but also bear their taunts, lashes and even daggers and swords. Why don't you let us know about that authority? Don't you want us to be among the blessed by following the exact rules taught by such claimants? Were such rules and regulations directly conferred upon them, or do they have any authority from you to devise and teach? Oh Lord, we are sure that you never will leave anyone stranded who sincerely wants to be guided by you. We are sure that you are absolute love and never refuse forgiveness to anyone who seeks it. We are seekers, we are humble, and we are downtrodden. Does our voice reach you from beneath your heavy weights while they are shouting in uncountable numbers? Though they do not let us speak, we are sure that you listen to unspoken words also. We are sure that you love the suppressed, weak voices more than the pompous loud ones. You are the

Chatha Ghulam

Lord of the weak and humble, you are the Lord of every human being and not only of great numbers, so we should not worry. Wherever we are, we are in your kingdom and have faith in your justice. We need not worry as you are Almighty and our Lord the God, the God."

THE DAY OF JUDGMENT
(A PERSONAL VIEW)

Oh, the hustle and bustle, astounded humans running in bewilderment and panic, gathering in groups…though deeply perplexed, are saying:

"Oh, the Day has come and, we shall enjoy as we believe. Our clergies told us!"

"It seems that, that group is whispering about Paradise, but they are fools to speak of it."

"Both groups are silly, how pleasant it will be when both will be dammed and pushed to Hell. They will repent and wish to be one of us, but now it is of no use."

"Though they are in big groups, we are sure that only our worship of the God will be accepted, and they will be declared heathen."

"This is the Day we have been denying, but this is the reality and life was actually a dream. We are astonished that we took that dream as the only reality."

"Oh, there are so many groups, many which became extinct, and many we are not even aware of."

"Don't bother, our Great Holiness (personality) is about to appear and we are sure to get into Paradise."

"Foolish fellows, their Great Holiness has to ask permission from ours, and ours certainly will not grant it for their not believing in him."

"The God promised that only the followers of our Great Holiness will be blessed with heaven, and the God will authorize him to recommend heaven to whom-so-ever he likes."

"Fie on them, they have been undergoing the ordeal of worship and gained nothing. Had they followed our way, this day would not have been heavy upon them."

SUDDEN LIGHT. BIG LIGHT. MUCH TOO BIG TO DESCRIBE. ALL ARE HELD IN AMAZEMENT. THEY TRY TO COLLECT THEIR SENSES BUT DO NOT RECOVER FULLY!

"Lord, we have been fighting for you and your Great Holiness and killed many who were non-believers and hostile to us."

"Lord, they are the liars. We have been fighting against them to establish the supremacy of your real Great Holiness and we believe that for our Great Holiness you created the universe and we have been offering sacrifices of our lives."

"Lord, they are the proud and never followed the correct way of worship. We deserve your blessings."

"Lord, we are here, order them to get aside and make way for us."

"Lord, none of them called or invited us sincerely to have a faith in you, so we remained obstinate and inflexible."

A VOICE, A DEEP BOTTOMLESS PROFOUND VOICE COMES FROM FAR AND NEAR, IS HEARD BUT NOT EXACTLY DEFINED.

"Humans, you are divided into many groups; each one is a claimant of Paradise which has no limits. The tastes you never tasted, endless joys and luxuries which you never experienced are all everlasting. Had you all been not stubborn, proud and defiant, this Paradise would have accommodated all of you and even then, this would have seemed to you extremely spacious. I am your creator and I created you of one nature and required all of you to be of one faith; but because of your selfish wishes to gain superiority over one another you divided yourselves into groups. I have already promised not to allow the blessings of this Paradise to the proud and to all proud claimant groups because they divided one easy and simple faith, twisted it according to their desires, invented many complications and unnecessary ceremonies. I did not want to put you in such difficulties, but you evolved and tried to impose them unjustly on yourselves and others. You are to be pushed into Hell, which I have created for the proud, wicked and cruel. Such is the just punishment for non-believers such as you. You consumed your lives and missed opportunities to repent; but now it is of no use because you have clearly seen your end-result and my providence. Now you will not be doing so by your own free will. You did not pay heed to advice by my declared and undeclared messengers. They did not demand any reward from you for themselves but only for you to believe and have faith in me and no more. You killed unjustly, spread hatred, were not merciful and did not feed the hungry. The less wicked will get less punishment and your leaders or those crueler will have to undergo the more severe as they justly deserve. It was and is so easy for me to be thoroughly aware of the minutest detail of your actions and intentions individually or in groups.

"Look, there are some patient, uncomplaining, serene and wise people. They are not claiming, but hopeful, and I have promised not to ever leave such people dejected. They are not part of your divisions and they are not proud of their group or any group. They are only mine and their faith is for me only without any conditions or preoccupation. In me only they trust. They are not proud of any Great except me. They worshiped me, they loved me, were never proud of their purity, never tried to impose their likes over those of others, placed themselves or any other between me and my people as you did. They loved mankind and did not hate anyone. They fought, but only to protect the innocent or weak from the atrocities of the aggressive and cruel. All of you individually or collectively did have the ability and opportunity to behave as they did, but you did not. You were reminded many times, but you did not heed. Why have you imposed restrictions on yourself and other people to join your group and act as you liked for my blessings? Was I bound to you, or have you ever received such a promise from me? No.

"Oh, my believers, you are mine, so I am yours. Peace is for you. This place of utmost joy and satisfaction is for you. You felt my presence though you never saw me, believed and then remained loyal. I have pardoned your mistakes. Now you are worthy of such a prestigious place, Paradise. There you will instantly get all the delights and joys you wish for. The Devil and his colleagues cannot enter, so they don't bother to try. In Paradise you will not have even the slightest worry. You will certainly pray and thank your God for blessing you with such a prize."

THE CHRIST YOU BELIEVE

It was perhaps midnight. I was half asleep, half awake and I had a dream.

There are dreadful clergies of mosques and minarets shouting-loudly at the God. It seems as if they will catch hold of him. They are bent upon smashing, threshing, whipping and killing the dissenters or non-believers in the name of God. The horrible clergies push others into hell and save heaven for themselves. They will be blessed for their job if they will not allow the God and his belongings to be desecrated by others. They are enthusiastic and excited to be guards for the God. How cruel they might be for the purpose though they also say that the God is almighty and merciful.

There are followers of the Christ. They are also proud to be his followers, but are they his or is he theirs? Do they not wear the cross when torturing or misbehaving with others? Perhaps they put it aside and wear it again later because it would have reminded them of the crucifixion of the Christ. They could not have tortured, misbehaved or done anything wrong with others while wearing the cross. They say that the Christ is love, but are they really Christians? So many Christians, so many blessed people. The God is Almighty and, I dare not challenge this thought. There are clergies of churches. Why do they walk so proudly? Do they not remember the time the Christ was being taken for crucifixion? Perhaps they forget, otherwise they would have been very humble and loving to all humans except the wicked and cruel. Perhaps the God has bestowed upon them authority of certification for blessings. Should I not send my blessings to anyone because I am not authorized and certified?

I shall fling open doors of churches and meet the Christ myself and then obey whatever He says. I shall attack although I am weak and alone –but I have a strong will. Oh no, the God is love, Christ is love, I claim to be a believer and follower, so violence and quarrelling is prohibited for me. Let them do their job and I mine. I can have my Christ without interfering in churches. My God, I am also your human. I think myself to be a follower of your Christ and you know that I am neither wicked nor cruel. I hope you will forgive me. I do not claim an entry into your heaven, just pardon me, my Lord.

The God might have created the Christ without any father and the Holy Mary was his mother. How did he do that? This is his business and none of mine as He created the first human without any father and without any mother. I respect the Christ and Mary without any reservations.

I PRAYED TO THE GOD

I prayed to the God to accept me as His.

"My God, I am not fit to be yours so please shape me as you wish. I know there may be hardships and naturally I shall ask your favors while facing such hardships. If such hardships are necessary to make me more acceptable to you, do not grant me those favors and continue shaping me just as a good surgeon continues operating and does not release his patient even if he feels pain. My God, you know that I am weak and, I may crumble, so provide me energy to face all the processing. You are the Merciful and you can do so without giving me more pain; but I do not want to be rejected by you at any cost. Take me and do whatever you want. I surrender all my attachments, whatever they are. I am Akbar as my parents named me, otherwise I am nothing but your creation, your human and yours only."

WISDOM VS IGNORANCE

There might be various definitions of wisdom or only one agreed upon, but allow me to define wisdom in my own words. Human nature on which the God demands humans to behave or act is supreme, but it is very often contaminated with self-righteousness in all fields of life including religion. I think the ability to distinguish self-righteousness from supreme human values in words and deed, is wisdom. One who possesses such ability is indeed a wise man or woman. There might be sublime, moderate, less, or no wisdom and adverse or negative wisdom. Adverse or negative wisdom is ignorance and, similarly there is more or. less ignorance as the case may be. Knowledge of all sorts is good, but a scholar, religious or not, may not be wise. An illiterate person may have gained wisdom blessed by the God, by pondering on the universe, creation and the creator.

I think that a human who can differentiate between selfish wishes or desires and truth or justice is a wise human. What he speaks out on the basis of such truth and justice, if not contaminated with selfish wishes or desires, is wisdom.

This wisdom empowered by a faith in the God makes high human values. In fact, faith in the God is a basis of such wisdom. Humans with sublime wisdom are known or unknown saints. Saints undoubtedly have sublime wisdom.

Some people call disparity between self-righteousness and truth a clash between flesh and spirit. This might be between flesh and spirit, devil and human, but no doubt there is a conflict going on and I define it as the difference between wisdom and ignorance. Wisdom never fights against wisdom, while ignorance clashes against wisdom and ignorance itself. Wisdom can defend itself if ignorance attempts to crush or harm it. Some people also name various wisdoms such as political, military and business wisdom. This is professionalism and concerned humans are experts of their respective fields, but they may not be wise.

Let sense prevail and not selfish wishes. If wisdom prevails, there will be harmony, love and peace; and if ignorance prevails, there will be destruction, hatred and cruelty. The wise necessarily require freedom of thought and cannot be detained by compulsions or regulations, religious or not. Wisdom is light and ignorance is darkness. Wisdom is Godly and ignorance is un-Godly.

HUMANS AND ANIMALS

I heard some news on television that scientists have proved that ninety-nine point four percent similarities in the genes of chimpanzees and humans. I have also heard about Darwin's theory of evolution. Does this mean that all religions are human made and that there aren't any saints or prophets? Does this mean that there isn't any God and the creation of the universe is an accidental process? Does this mean that the human values we talk about are, in fact, animal values and the rule of "the survival of the fittest" prevails?

I have not read many books, so I think that you people will help me be aware of some basic questions.

Why is there so much visible behavioral difference if there is 99.4% resemblance?

Can a scientist create? Can there be any species in between humans and the nearest parallel animals so that resemblance is merely accidental?

When did that so-called change take place? Did that change take place simultaneously all over the globe? I think such a change could not have happened simultaneously and if the change was not simultaneous, there would have been some species having more resemblance to animals and some with humans. Why aren't there such mixed human-animals and animal-humans?

Did humans ever live mixed up with such animals in known history or are there only presumptions? Can there be any blood change among humans and such animals? If not, why do all humans have one kind of blood and any other species' blood does not match with it? As far as I know all humans can interchange blood.

I think that the Creator created life and life resembles other life including humans, birds and all animals. All eat, excrete, have sex and reproduce. All feel pleasure, pain, happiness and anxiety. Such common things cause scientists and other scholars to point out similarities. These, no doubt exist, but there isn't and cannot be any human-like species except mankind.

WHY PRIESTS, MONKS, NUNS DO NOT MARRY?

I have many times heard in the news that some priests have been accused of raping children. Is marriage or sex prohibited for them?

I think to prohibit this is unnatural and unnecessary for spirituality. Why deny nature? The God created this attraction. I think that the God does not require humans to curb this desire unnecessarily. In my country there are many restrictions imposed by religion and unjust social traditions so there are honor killings and many men and women living without marriage - also without sex though they do not wish to. This is extremism, suppression and violation of basic human rights.

Various religions observe fasting on particular days of the year. The basic philosophy behind such practices is that humans should be grateful to their God for giving them such blessings such as food and water. If a human is already suffering from the shortage of food and water, why should he fast? I know that most people who observe fasting are not grateful to the God, but perform the fast only as a ceremonial religious duty. The God does not want them to be hungry or thirsty without any purpose. I think that there are no restrictions concerning eating and drinking, only to like or dislike, be clean and not dirty, and practice good hygiene. Some laws regarding drugs do matter. The sexual desire need not be curbed unnecessarily. Extreme hunger, thirst and sexual desire must be satisfied if possible before any spiritual practice, otherwise there will not be reality and hypocrisy will result. Like all other blessings, humans should be grateful to the God for this.

I do realize that some moralities have to be observed regarding traditions, ethics and human values, but I think that a state or religion should not interfere or impose regulations unless there is raping or sex by force. Raping and sex by compulsion should be punished and that punishment may differ from case to case according to state laws.

Why do religions demand that priests, monks and nuns not practice sex, a God-given desire and joy? Do they not feel it severely? Does this not divert their attention? I am not aware of some religious or church traditions, and I hope you will not mind my questions.

EXPECTING MIRACLES

EXPECTING MIRACLES

My friends, I have been explaining my feelings on various subjects regarding faith in the God. No doubt miracles are from the God only and I am human just like you. Some or many of you might be more knowledgeable than I, but I have some feelings about miracles, so allow me to express them.

Miracles do not happen on demand from humans. They do not happen in ordinary circumstances, nor did they happen only in certain times in history. They are not time bound. If a man jumps into the sea by his own will and expects a miracle to happen to save his life, he is totally in the wrong and misled; but if is a believer and forcibly pushed into the sea, may hope for the God's help. I mean the God may help in unavoidable dangers but not in those created. A believer does not lose hope, but hope is hope and should never be taken for granted. A true believer might be blessed with a miracle by the God. Miracles happen in extreme danger or under extreme circumstances because one has to be extremely passionate in calling out to the God for help. Such passionate calling even in silence might result in a miracle. Patience is necessary.

Some chosen persons might be blessed with one or more miracles by the God. This blessing is never granted to be exercised as a magic show and blessed personalities should be very humble when miracles happen through them by the will of the God. Magic has its base in pride and defiance, but miracles do not happen without humbleness and utter submissiveness to the God. Magicians feel pride in their performance while believers pray to the God if they are blessed with any miracle. Humbleness is necessary for sincere prayers. They should not take any miracle as their own doing.

There are miracles which we take as routine matter. Some of us might have experienced narrow escapes, but we don't think of them as coming from somewhere other than ourselves and are not grateful to the God. In fact, all good happenings, including our lives and health are blessings of the God, if not miracles. Let us pray for such miracles which bring peace, love and satisfaction among humans. I believe faith in the God can bring such good changes.

IS THE GOD UNJUST?

Many or all religions believe that there is a God. Some religions believe that there are also other gods beside the God. We are not concerned with such gods, but with the God only. Almost all religions believe that the God is absolutely-just and that humans with all their good intentions can slip or mistake justice. The God being the Almighty does practice justice in the absolute. There are some questions in my mind, or may be in yours, challenging the justness of the God. Please cooperate and join hands to give suitable answers to that faith in the God does not shatter or weaken. I am not a learned scholar or a philosopher, so I need your help. Please help me in the name of God.

Somebody said (God forbid) that the God is cruel, that He allows some of his followers the choice to conquer, suppress and even kill their opponents. He is very happy if such a group is successful, but if others harm them or even intend to do so, He is annoyed. Is this not cruelty that He does not bother about humans who don't belong to his so-called special group?

Somebody said (God forbid) that the God is class conscience and He feels happy when nobles or the wealthy arrange special majestic ceremonies in his honor. The upper class can pray in a befitting manner while the poor cannot and, the poor even have unbefitting places to worship. Is this not class consciousness?

Somebody said (God forbid) that the God accepts bribery. A wealthy person might give alms in God's name. Wealth is required to perform pilgrimages or other religious bindings. Wealth is also required to please renowned clergies so they will pray for God's blessings. Some powerful influential persons make some clergies pray for them in the most holy places declared by the God while the poor remain deprived. Does the God accept bribery?

Somebody said (God forbid) that the God is unjust in providing luxuries of life to some people while others remain suffering. Resources are necessary in every field of life and the poor die for want of medicine, shelter, food. How can they pray to the God sincerely when feeling such agitations in their hearts?

Somebody said, and this time he seemed much more confident, (God forbid) that the God is surely unjust for blessing some people with his true religion and, keeps depriving others of the knowledge of that religion. How can natives of new-found lands or people who lived before the advent of that blessed religion be blamed for not believing? Nearly a century ago more than half the population of this globe was not aware of proclaimed religions. Even among these religions only one is said to be true. Can any ordinary person living constantly in a huge community without any opportunity to travel to other regions think about any change, if his religion is not a blessed one? Is the God ignoring merit and equality for allowing only his so-called preferred group to enter heaven? Will only that group be blessed as a whole, while others will be damned as a whole? Is this not injustice?

Please join hands to answer these questions. I believe that these are totally unjust charges against the God. Please be serious and sincere because if such charges are not successfully and undoubtedly refuted, there will be no room for any religion. Please think, if the God is unjust, how can any religion be justified? I think most people are indifferent towards religions especially in the modern world, although apparently they seem to be. I appeal to you for your help despite your religious attachments.

THE GOD IS JUST

If the God is unjust there cannot be comparison of any sort. If the God is unjust, let there be no values, no mercy, no kindness, no charities and no ethics. If the God is unjust, why do not humans avail every opportunity for their personal pleasures and progress? Might it be that it would be at the cost of others' blood and sufferings? The God is absolutely just. The God created us so there are human values not necessarily to be interpreted by religious clergies. Believers of the God have sublime human values because they have faith in the God and therefore in His values also. They keep these values whatever conditions or circumstances may be.

Self-righteous religious leaders teach their followers that their God wants them to establish the supremacy of their religion and in doing so they suppress, plunder and kill others. They also preach that their God will reward them for this and if any of them loses his life, will be instantly received in heaven. There is no such unjust God, so please do not attach such labels with the God as He, the merciful, is the God of humans not of religions. If any group or groups believe their God is cruel and unjust, then their God is untrue and does not exist. No doubt the God loves brave people who fight against cruelty, inequality, suppression, hatred and social injustice and those who provide protection of the weak against unjust aggressors. Such people are heroes or martyrs regardless of their religious attachments.

Selfish humans always want to excel above others and have special privileges in every field of life including religion or religious ceremonies. They manifest their pride to be coveted by others. They do not have activities to please the God, but to please themselves, concerned clergies and, those humans who do not have faith in the God. The God does not care for such ceremonies and true believers are not impressed by such frail activities. Majestic places of worship are also not built to please the God but to satisfy their delusions of wealth just as palaces or other pretentious buildings are. Humbleness is necessary to pray to the God and if majestic places cause the loss of humbleness, there can be no prayers.

The God likes quality and not quantity. His quality standards are Godly. He may like a bit of bread given to another hungry person by a hungry person, who himself had not sufficient to satisfy his own hunger more than tons of food given by a wealthy person in alms. The clergies' ranking, repute and influence are not awarded by the God, and a layman can be dearer to him than the highest position holders of any religion. Sincerity of feelings is necessary for praying and ceremonial prayers without feelings of attachment to concerned persons are merely ceremonial and not actually prayers. Pilgrimages to so-called holy places are unnecessary if faith in the God is not enhanced. A person not participating in any pilgrimage may have more faith in the God than one who does. The whole universe is holy as it is God's manifestation. So, the poor need not worry about pleasing clergies or performing pilgrimages. The God does not demand interference of clergies of any religion in granting forgiveness to humans. In fact, it totally depends on the sincerity of repentance and does not matter who or where the concerned human is.

Does wealth bring satisfaction or happiness? I have seen many rich people who feel gloomy, lonely and depressed to the point of committing suicide. I have also seen many poor living happily and, enjoying life more than many rich. I think we all have heard stories of love in which one partner leaves a luxurious life to live with a partner. No doubt they do it for happiness for which wealth is not necessary. No doubt sincerity in all human relations including family and friends gives happiness and satisfaction. The wealthy also sometimes wish to live a simple, natural, peaceful life. The God wants the rich not to spend wealth on superfluous luxuries but to provide the poor with the necessities of life. He warns them that if they do not behave properly, He will deprive them of happiness and satisfaction even though they have much wealth. In life after death they also have to suffer. Humans bring miseries to themselves by their own doing. Affected by pride and selfishness they fight, cheat, betray and grab. Such activities bring suffering including illness and a shortage of necessities. Had they been soft-hearted, loving and kind to each other, being believers of the God, they would have been certainly relieved and rewarded by the God. Believers of the God can and surely live satisfied lives without luxuries.

Whoever seeks the God whole-heartedly surely finds Him. Followers of various religions don't actually seek guidance but, demand it from the God and it must be according to their cherished religion with prescribed boundaries taught by their respective clergies. Demanding guidance from the Almighty with preconditions is totally improper. Seeking guidance requires utter submission, surrendering all racial, linguistic, regional and religious attachments and giving up all personal liking/disliking. If a human loves God above all attachments, then he/she is surely blessed with guidance. I request clergies of all religions to free humanity and to not set conditions. No human can seek the God if he is not personally sincere, no matter to which religion he is attached. No special prayers, manner of prayer, special places of prayer are necessary to pray to the God. He demands humbleness, truthfulness and sincerity and does not care much about manners or group attachment. All humans are basically equal, no matter in which age they lived. All have equal opportunity to have faith in the God. Unlike religions, faith in the God is not a heritage.

The God is just and no qualification should be attached to his name as many religion holders or self-righteous humans attempt to do to satisfy their selfish wishes.

FAITH VS RELIGIONS

My friends, I hope you will not mind if I say faith is liberalism and religions are fundamentalism because religions persist on their righteousness while faith does not. Faith draws no boundaries and it has no limits while religions have their demarked boundaries and have limitations. Religions have certified authorities which admit or expel followers. Their followers have to be cautious of the limitations imposed on them. Therefore, I believe, they are not free people. Faith does not accept any authority other than the God and does not claim any ownership of the God and not even preference of any sort. Religions do claim such preferences violating a basic right of equality among humans. Religions cause divisions which the God does not like, while faith unites humanity as it is comprised of love, mercy and equality of all humans not considering their racial, regional, traditional, linguistic and all other attachments.

Religions strive to maintain their different identities. Different shapes of worship places exhibit differentiation from others and only those who agree are allowed to enter. This is a matter of authority over God and his worship. Separate manners of worship are enforced upon followers and they are also taught words of worship. Clergies also stress on different appearances like hair and dress. Different times of worship are observed with different modes. Most religions have different names to show their so-called superiority over others as, they do not want to be mixed up with the others. Most heinous of crimes have been committed in the name of religion and most deadly wars were fought to please their God or gods. Apart from other religions, Christian persecution by Jews, Jew persecution by Christians including the Holocaust, Muslim, Hindu, Sikh massacres in the Indian sub-continent, including those of 1947, are very good examples of religious beliefs.

Unlike religions, faith is not concerned with differentiations but with the

God and humanity. Faith does not need any particular place for worship as, the God can be prayed to anywhere not depending upon the shape of a building. Faith can be practiced anywhere whether or not it is a religious place because it is something which comes from within and not from any orthodox religious teaching. Faith does not recognize any authority between the God and humanity and if there is one, it should be abolished. There must not be any intervention between a lover and the beloved. Faith does not require any special mannerisms for being accepted, but if it does require something, it is a firm and staunch belief in the God. Does a lover need to be taught manners of love, or would he or she like such restrictions? Submission and obedience to the God also does not necessarily need particular words to be repeated by all. He does not want or like such submission as He is not an army general seeking only disciplined speech. He likes to be prayed to willingly, with love and sincerity; and sincere, obedient lovers by nature know manners of love, remembering, asking and praying. There may be prayers even without spoken words. The God knows feelings of hearts and, values feelings much more than words. All names are good which have good meaning regardless of language or religious background. Is there any God of time or day? No. All times and days are God's and He wants humans to remember him at all times and on all days. The God hates cruel, wicked, unjust aggressors disregard of any attachment including those religious, as He is the God of humans and not of groups.

Faith unites humanity and promotes love among families, friends, races and nations. A true faith in the God must promote love wherever it exists, otherwise it will be untrue and fake. Faith is love; the God loves humanity and wants humans to be faithful.

Spirituality will survive while religions change and become extinct. Spirituality is actual and real liberalism which provides liberty to the soul that religions deny.

Spirituality is universal and covers the beginning of time to eternity while religions are time-bound having a beginning and, also an end. Religions have necessary connections with special ceremonies to feed upon while spirituality is free from all such encumbrances. Spirituality gets its nourishment directly from the soul so, thereby there is no fear of it being severed from its roots.

COMMON FAITH

Join me or allow me to join,
I may be yours if you are not mine,
The God of yours is God of mine,
I can pray at any or without a shrine.

Traditions change and customs change,
Dialects change and languages change,
People migrate and nations change,
Wars and calamities bring drastic change.

Religions change with clergy's behavior,
As he explains to win peoples favor,
Poor get rich if lucky and clever,
Humans don't change and humanity never.

You are a human and I am a human,
Don't you think we have much in common?
Our goods are common and our vices common,
Our values are common and our humanity common.

Our God is common and Creator common,
He made us common and we are common,
Let us love and love is common,
Let us say our faith is common.

RELIGION VERSUS RELIGIONS

The God is one, but religions differ and, they (God forbid) compel the God to be theirs only. Each claims the God's preference. Each claims to have God's authority or (God forbid) authority over God. Faith in the God including mercy, kindness, love, justice, brotherhood, fraternity and good social behavior does not fulfill the need to have a separate religion so some or more additions, conditions and other specialties are necessary requirements. Religions require clergies to teach such specialties and clergies rely on specialties of the concerned religion for their existence. How can clergies say that theirs can be no way other than observance of such specialties?

All religions join in such competition so separate additions, conditions, and other manners are included for keeping entities separate. Claims of superiority are necessary to satisfy respective followers. Each religion claims to have the best additions and conditions. Places of worship, manners and times of worship and observance of holy days, pilgrimages to holy places and observance of traditions from birth to death and even the names of individuals are kept for maintenance of religious differences. I know some clergies who insist on observing particular-manners for eating, drinking, walking, sleeping entering a building or coming out of it. They also insist on related prayers for all such occasions to be learned by heart. Religions must be unique by having to have different holy personalities for attaining blessings and for receiving approvals to enter heaven.

Clergies of each religion claim that heaven or blessings of the God are only for their followers excluding all others. This can be a perfect base for scuffles and, also wars. Somewhere in holy books followers are admonished to not be friendly with others and they are motivated to wage holy wars against those who do not accept their God. I appreciate the wisdom of all religious followers who do not fight in-spite of having such obvious differences. They live in peace on the principle of live and let live. Does this mean that they have turned hypocrite?

Please allow me to point out some hypocrisy (as I think). Please forgive me if I am wrong. People of many religions believe that there is an endless life after death with unimaginable pleasures, satisfaction and happiness. Such life is invisible. I think that had there been a visible life just equal to this life we are living; people would have given more importance to such a life. People do prefer to live with ease in a hope for future and for this purpose they save, work and even suffer. Had there been a visible transformation from one place to another, people would have been more concerned that such time would be at least equal or better than their present life. If this is correct then hypocrisy certainly exists – otherwise why do they not care much for that endless life? Why do they cheat, torture, kill and lie? Why do they remain cruel and unkind? This certainly means that they do not believe in that endless life and despite that their religions do accept their eligibility for heaven and blessings of their God above all other humans not belonging to their creed or group. If you do not mind, this seems to me hypocrisy.

I do believe in life after death and that the human soul will never perish. I also believe in the God's rewards and punishments, but I do not claim to have achieved perfection in faith.

IF IN THE NAME OF GOD

If in the name of God you fight,
If in the name of God you kill,
Will He hold you up by his might?
Will He favor you by his will?

He is their God also as others claim,
Had He been yours as you say,
Why at times do you bear shame?
Why do you suffer as others may?

So better not on him rely,
So better not him to call,
Call to yours, if they reply,
Yours only don't like you to fall.

Fight in names of yours you believe,
Kill in names of yours not others,
They will favor you if not asleep,
Or have knowledge and any powers.

THE GOD AND ATTACHMENTS

Every object living or not has some connection to some other object. These objects can be called attachments and they get importance according to the original object and, if the original object is taken as hostile or bad, the objects of affection are also taken as such according to their category. If the original object is taken as good, the concerned fascination is also taken as such according to its level and category.

There are also non-living attachments and objects. A gift presented by a beloved friend, or a meeting point associated with him/her may bring fond memories, so these also become a secondary part of that love. Similarly, a dagger with which anybody's beloved was slain becomes a part of hatred. No doubt attachments have their effect on the human mind and, they depend upon original objects for their importance, if they are detached, become valueless.

I believe all religions have one object as a center of their devotion called the God. These objects consist of the living or inanimate whether they are persons, places or things. The difference of these appendages and how they are regarded make religions. Self-righteous human groups claim to have or, own connections that have superiority over those of others. They also claim that because they have indispensable superior charm, the God also prefers them. Attachments are never indispensable, especially when all-time availability and presence of the real object is guaranteed.

To have a regard and love for attachments is not bad. Such a love can be a symbol of great love for the original object. Idols cannot be taken as real especially when the real object, the God, is present. Since the God is omnipresent, an attachment, living or not, doesn't matter much.

Within the jurisdiction of every religion, anybody can speak freely about the God without annoying others, except if the comment is adverse or detrimental to the religion or their particular attachment. This means that attachments are not a necessary source of enhancement of faith in the God, but impediments in the way to God.

The God blessed all humans with a common nature called human values. Good humans, believers of the God, have and observe sublime human values naturally whether, or not they have religion. A faith in the God does not require humans to quarrel over their beloved belongings or their status. Those who do so are no doubt religious, but not faithful to the God. They strive to enhance the importance of attachments over the real object -- "the God." They are self-righteous and try to blur faith in the God under their religion and, their so-called idols and rituals. Clearing the way of any intervention is a pre-requisite for a faith in the God. No one should intervene between a lover and beloved, or a human and the God.

Unlike religion, faith in the God is not a heritage.

I WISH

Oh my God, I have many deficiencies. I do not and must not insist on my righteousness. I ask you for guidance and am happily willing to adopt whatever way you like without any reservations, likes or dislikes of mine. I totally submit myself to you willingly and to none else can I have such submission. I hope you will accept my plea. I am sincere. I am sure that you do not reject sincerity. I part with any person, group, land, or thing whatever that may be if you wish me to do that. I am yours and yours only. I wish that my loyalty to you is above all loyalties with persons and things which I have, or which can be dear to me in this universe of yours. I wish that none of my attachments is a hindrance between you and me.

Oh my God, I know that you can give me plenty of all joys. I do not wish them all, but if I might happen to wish extravagancies, I beg you not to give me special favor. You know what is good or bad for me, so I surrender all my wishes. I beg you to give me only that much which is good. You are Lord of honors and you bless honor. I do not wish an honor as it might become a source of pride for me. I know pride is hateful and you hate pride, so do not give me anything which brings this vice to me. I wish that I remain contented by your will. I wish justice, equality and love among humans. Up with love and down with hatred. I may err and wish for an injustice or inequality in favor of myself or my associates. Even then forgive me and do not fulfill any such wish. My Lord this will be your real favor to me and I beg for your favors. I am ignorant and do not really know what is favorable or unfavorable for me.

Oh my God, I believe that I am not going to be finished though I am growing old as everybody does. My life is not certain even for a day or a moment. I believe that you will not leave your good humans helpless and you will reward them. People say that you have a paradise of utmost joys, beyond imagination of humans. I believe that the most joyful feature will be your ultimate connection. I believe that there will not be any risk of my forgetting you, or not being yours anytime, any moment. I wish to meet you there. Forgive me my Lord if my wish is not appropriate. You are my Lord and to ask from you is my only right before you. I shall keep on asking for your blessings for all my life, as this is necessary for a relationship of servant to master.

LAWFUL VICES

My friends, I have always wanted to express my views on all aspects of life in the light of my faith. I do not claim that my views are perfect; but as a free human I think should do that because my views do not necessarily correspond with any particular religious binding. I think many religions include good human values. I believe faith in the God does teach human values without much learning from books, teachers or other sources. I hope you will correct me if I am wrong.

Almost all humans wish to get rich for their needs or extravagant luxuries, and they struggle for that purpose. There are many unlawful means which you people very well know and there are some lawful vices which any law may not cover. I think betraying anyone's faith for unjust profit, taking advantage of others' unavoidable needs or plight and, gambling are lawful social vices.

I think betrayal is universally considered bad, so there isn't any need for discussion. Profit or interest whatever the name may be is not in itself good or bad and a situation may differ from cast to case. You are aware of many unjust agreements between victorious and defeated nations, groups or persons. Such agreements might be binding, legal or mutually agreed upon, but they can be very unjust.

No justly negotiated agreement can be made with a thirsty person for providing water, with a hungry person for providing food, or with a person requiring medical care for himself or dears. The God wants humans to be kind, loving and helpful to the poor or needy. Helping persons should act as if it were their duty without taking advantage and, without any sense of supremacy. Such aid might be as a giver or as a receiver, if the needy are in position to repay after a certain period. Business loans and transactions do not fall under humanitarian needs so those are separate matters. A miser or an extravagant person is equally bad for a good society and so not liked by the God although they deal with their own lawful wealth. One hold back the God's blessings when should be beneficial and others spend them when they should be kept for a needier time. The God wants them to spend for the welfare of the suffering and needy humanity.

Gambling might be fun for rich persons or for persons of those countries who enjoy a well established social services system, but I think it also negatively affects their behavior. Believers take each and everything as the God's blessing and the God does not want humans to test Him. The God's favors are expected by believers in unavoidable circumstances that aren't self-created. The riches gained in gambling are not taken as blessings and are not spent for positive human requirements for self or others, so it is void of satisfaction. To a loser it might be a cause of despair because, they may not take it as a natural happening and be contented. They, themselves, are to be blamed and may not take it as the God's will. Despair might be the result. Despair is not liked by the God and it certainly has a negative social impact. I know that many gamblers in developing or under developed countries lose their homes and essential livelihoods for self and family. This is a very bad aspect of gambling and, losers sometimes commit suicide. Is the God, Nature, or luck to be blamed for such adverse circumstances? Such circumstances do not cause dejection, but despair. Dejection is neither Godly nor un-Godly, but despair is un-Godly.

Believers having faith in the God's mercy are satisfied by the God's will, but to lose in gambling is not the God's way. Gambling is a financial game, in which the gainer wins at the direct cost of the loser, so it differs from business. One's happiness may bring sorrow and suffering to another. Believers may not wish to win such selfish happiness, so I think it is morally banned for them. This may not be taken as the God's favor or blessing and is a social vice.

MORALE BOOSTING

Morale boosting has been in vogue from pre-historic days. People used to blow pipes, beat drums and sing songs for purpose of boosting morale. Such activities also boost up the morale of armies, civilizations and other groups based on races and religions. Almost all groups arrange yearly or occasional ceremonies to exhibit their pomp and show. Such functions help their groups to be united and retain their separate identities.

When a human baby comes into being, is a human and nothing more. Subsequently is taught about all grouping by concerned elders. That human is taught to have a separate history, traditions, language, race and religion. Such groups not only strive to maintain these distinctions but to prosper by an increase in number and numbers mean power, so they very justly require morale boosting.

We shall discuss here morale boosting of religions with reference to faith in the God. All religions make their followers believe that they only are to be blessed on a preferential basis even though they might not be more human than some other person. They arrange ceremonies in purposely built buildings daily, weekly, yearly or occasionally. Such buildings are also magnificently built to boost up morale of the worshipers. All groups try to hold such activities with full dignity because without such ceremonies their followers may lose morale. Religions sometimes arrange pilgrimages to their exclusive holy places to make sure their followers are adequately blessed. Big congregations certainly have an impact on the minds of participants.

Rhetoric by concerned clergies plays an important role as did rhetoric by Hitler to boost the morale of Germans. These clergies lay stress on religious preferences of their followers otherwise, they will not be accepted as clergies in their community and will certainly lose their jobs. Their ability to do so proves a scale of measurement for listing. Rhetoric is an art and ability which has been used by concerned group leaders and contributes greatly in successful grouping.

I am Muslim by birth. People used to say and believe that the Milky Way in the sky is the way on which the Prophet went one night to meet Allah. I also believed so in my childhood. I do not know whether people still believe it as I haven't discussed it. I believe that people are inclined to believe what they like to believe and, they are not inclined or willing to believe what they do not like to believe. All religions have many such wishful beliefs and are not willing to depart with those beliefs because those beliefs are necessary to boost morale and to keep their separate identities. They are always ready to accept that which gives them an edge over others. Propaganda and sources of communication are vital.

Finance helps a lot in morale boosting. Religions also allowed looting and collecting booties in wars as they were aware of the importance of monies gained from their stolen goods. This is a fact that power and finance changed the religions of many and, are still very effective. People are very impressed by power and wealth and do not like to pray in poorly built places of worship.

I believe that all these morale-boosting activities and beliefs are to block the way of true faith and, have to be removed before one can seek guidance from the God. This morale boosting is actually, pride boosting. Humbleness is necessary to seek guidance. Morale boosting leads humans to be proud and provides a basis for belonging. There should be no pride, no such grouping. No real faith has any sort of pride. The God is the God of the universe, the God of humans and not of religions, communities, so who-so-ever claims preferences from general humanity is definitely unfaithful. Sometimes people plunge into depression when they lose their pride and distinction based on riches, power, race or religion. Only a true faith in the God provides deep contentment which may never be shattered under any circumstance. True faith seeks shelter under the benevolence of God Almighty who never disappoints.

Sometimes morale boosting is used for good purposes and can be used to provide relief to oppressed, down trodden, helpless, weak or depressed persons. This is on human grounds to provide hope. Sincere and selfless help gives much relief. The best morale boosting is to help a concerned person to have faith in the God's benevolence and thereby beating depression very effectively. The needy should also be helped materially.

GIVE AND TAKE OF SINS

I think that religions include many absurdities with which faith in the God may not agree, are irrational and unreasonable. I understand that Christian, Muslim, Jewish faiths have such beliefs that one or more holy personalities will take their sins making them eligible to enter heaven. They also claim that certain personalities will recommend their so-called group and their recommendation will definitely be accepted by the God. Hindus believe that their sins can be washed away by bathing in holy waters of the River Ganges. I am not sure, but I think there is such a case with other religions such as Buddhist. I know about a belief of some religions including Muslim and perhaps Christian that giving prayers and blessings to somebody else living or dead will add to his account.

Are sins a commodity? If so, how big is sin? Is not every person responsible for his own actions? If sins are to be taken by others, why fear the God and why ask for His forgiveness?

How many sins will be taken by concerned personalities or washed in water and how many would be left? If all sins are to be taken, then why should the cruel or wicked fear damnation?

Will those who recommend, be committing injustice for recommending heaven for their concerned group as a whole including the bad, and deprive others from their due merit? Wouldn't some humans of those damned communities be better humans than the so-called blessed?

Who of these personalities is entitled, as every group rejects claims of all others? If a human does not happen to be aware of those entitled persons or of the cleansing powers of holy waters, why would be damned for no fault of his/her own? Is this not an injustice by the God?

Some religions believe that a human baby is born with sin. Is not such a God an unjust one who holds an infant born sinful when he has not yet attained the age of sensibility to discern between good and evil?

I think that a baby is born in the God's image and by nature is inclined to have a faith in the God, if not mislead by his elders or entangled in selfish pride on the base of religion. Don't you see that almost all nations happen to have a faith in an unseen power

I think if such questions are not properly answered, people will grow indifferent towards religion.

"THANKS GOD"

"Thanks God" is a very good prayer, if not only said, but felt. In fact all prayers relate to feelings and sincerity and lip service does not matter. The God knows with how much sincerity words are uttered, and even unspoken, He knows feelings of hearts and measures sincerity.

I believe that if a person is extremely hungry, he wants and wishes food, if thirsty, wants water, not rich food or packed drinks. Similarly, if he is facing severe weather, he wants clothing and shelter and not fashion costumes or luxurious living. When relieved he continues to add wishes, but all the God wants from him is contentment. What is the scale where anybody should be satisfied? This scale is minimum human requirements. Though struggling for more may not be prohibited, feeling discontent for not having much is not liked by the God. Learn to be content, pray and thank God for what you have.

If anybody has more than his just needs and happens to meet or know about someone not having minimum requirements, if is a believer, must help that person in the name of God. A barefooted person needs shoes and a naked body needs clothing; should not be choosy if provided with shoes and dress. He/she might feel restless and want more or that of higher quality. If is a believer, would be grateful to the God and say thanks to the God.

Let me quote one of many real examples. A family happened to live among neighbors, relatives and friends. This family became richer than the others and purchased a new luxury vehicle which the others didn't or couldn't have, so they were very happy and perhaps proud. Others envied their fortune. That family went out on a happy trip, but alas, suffered casualties. Those who escaped death very sadly said, "Had the God not given them that vehicle, they would not have suffered." I think is much better to be ever satisfied, as the God knows who will be lucky or unlucky. To be rich is not bad, but to be impatient for wealth and envious of others who are wealthy is not good. Be satisfied, be merciful, help others, and be not anxious to have more, enjoy calmness and say, "thanks, God." Let me say "thanks God" means contentment and happiness.

Riches do not necessarily bring happiness but, helping others surely does. Thank God that He gave you much to give and not to receive. Do not take wealth as your right. I believe that if all prayers are ceremonial, a praying person is not really thankful to the God and does not feel thankful to the God in his heart.

I believe the God does not want humans to suffer, but He wants them to remember and keep in mind that they may suffer in various ways and may lose various blessings, so be thankful to the God. Alas, mankind does not understand and does not say, "Thanks, God" when they suffer or, are relieved from sufferings.

COLLECTIVENESS AND FAITH

Yearning for collectiveness is common in almost all living beings. Yearning to live among fellow human beings is very strong among humans. Many humans living alone long to meet other humans, but almost all humans happen to live in societies and have their other preferences. Those who have some or more common grounds wish to live among others. These preferences and common grounds are based on various factors, some being race, religion or tradition.

Faith in the God does not negate these common factors, if they do not provide a base of pride for claiming supremacy over others. Pride on a base of any such factors is definitely a hurdle in the way of faith and the sense of collectiveness often enhances these factors. I believe religions very often change sincerity in ceremonials and devotees concentrate more on observance of manners instead of heart-felt feelings in their prayers.

A sense of sincerity in togetherness mitigates the effects of sorrow. It also heightens feelings of bliss and pleasure. A sorrowful person yearns to meet those who share a common sorrow, or at least understand his sorrow or suffering and can console him. In moments of happiness also, people like to be among those who may share their happiness. Such sharing gives much satisfaction.

Collectiveness also provides consolation and satisfaction and might evoke or boost faith among the faithful. Like all humans, the faithful also wish to meet other faithful like good seeks good. I believe such yearning was the basis of collective prayer, so there developed daily, weekly and yearly routine prayers. Also, I believe that with the passage of time such prayers became ceremonial, void of sincere feelings. Sincere group request deepens feelings of those who are asking therefore, collectiveness has its legitimacy in faith. I also believe that sincere expression of heart-felt feelings is liked by the God.

Places were also required for such community gatherings. Such places are called worship places. Buildings of such places were also a legitimate requirement. With the passage of time, religions built such buildings different from each other to keep their separate identities, and they also built magnificently almost as a contest to out-do each other. They also thought that they were pleasing their God or gods by spending more and glorifying such places.

I yearn to meet someone who'll at least allow me free expression in their presence. I shall feel much consoled in the company of those having similar views. Collective similarity of views based on sincerity provides consolation. Indeed, suppression is hard for humans with free thoughts even though they may feel content by the God's will.

THE RETREATING RELIGIONS AND TRADITIONS

Humans have made considerable progress in science, technology and have also gained much needed personal liberties. Religions and traditions have been and are continually retreating. There were unjust traditions that humans renounced in order to get their due freedom. I believe that many positive traditions have also been renounced. Such traditions may differ from region to region and community to community but are harmless and charming. These traditions provide the basis of human configuration, without which humans are becoming more commercial and materialistic.

Not all traditions are good. When there is a reaction, traditions do not stand in their actual desirable position but retreat, losing ground to materialism. Pure scientific approach in every field and aspect of life brings restlessness, hastiness and discontentment because it is entirely based on material gains and losses. The concept of competition devoid of any moral base causes dissatisfaction and, also dejection.

Had religions been on solid, realistic, natural footings, they would have resisted this reactive tendency. They were also oppressive, aggressive so they withdrew. Christian clerics enjoyed undue aggressive powers and when requested to do so, did not relinquish them willingly. Now they are losing their position on some matters such as homosexuality. Some of their groups are still denying the natural and just right of marriage for their clerics (male or female). Hindus have been practicing the caste system which may not be applicable on human or natural grounds. Their religion includes many good teachings and spirituality but, in many cases causes total renunciation. Muslim religious laws such as, death sentence for converters from Islam to any other religion; and a beating to death for unmarried sex couples; no music; no commingling with the opposite sex at any time; the cutting off of hands as theft punishment; -- forced prayers and allowing Muslims to attack and subjugate other nations are rarely practiced. Why do they not practice it if they believe it? Are they hypocrites or not sincere believers? I know that Islam has in it many good teachings but, the questions mentioned need to be settled and answered. Similarly, Jews, Buddhists and other religions have their specialties which don't conform to human nature. I believe that all religions have many unnatural unjust beliefs so, they have retreated.

Why are "true" believers who believe in the fundamentals of religions called fanatics yet, religions are believed to be true?

I believe that actual faith in the God never changed its position from the very beginning of humanity and is valid for all humans, the world and for all times. Pure faith is an eternal attraction for human souls and provides hope and contentment for all.

People say that the world is rapidly changing and, I see a positive change of individual freedom especially where people are denied this God-given right. I also see many negative changes, devoid of good traditions (religious or non-religious), good values, living very physically and not being harmonious with nature. The commercial race is causing unnatural, inharmonious changes.

Commercialism in all aspects of life is causing unnatural changes in arts, music, literature, poetry and a natural habitation is being renounced. Music and folk poetry of every region which were soothing, polite, harmonious with nature and soul elevating have changed and are being changed to being cacophonous, abrupt, harsh, hasty and discomforting. Perhaps people say this change is poppycock. It rocks for the time being and being artificial, eventually withers. Pure arts, music and literature have a lasting purifying effect because they charm the soul. It may be enjoyed without any changes for ages. Being harmonious with nature it remains soothing for all times. People should be at liberty to enjoy what they like. This is only a comparison of artificial and natural.

The clergies of religions seem to lack harmony with nature. They are ceremonial, artificial, book-keepers, reciting and insisting on superficialities, distinctions and divisions. They are bound to limitations and the result is dullness. They offer the same ceremonial remedies for all and are not innovative. Faith in the God is naturally humble, loving, wise, helping, merciful, passive, soft and, a perfect remedy for all disturbed souls. Such qualities may not be planted in hearts by religious learning and teaching, so the clergies are losing natural attraction. How can a clergyman impart sincerity without sincerity in his own heart? There is a need for sincere contemplation on yearnings of the soul; otherwise fleshy, materialistic living will rot the climate without a natural fragrance. There must be need of faith and love for spiritual and natural nourishment of human souls, otherwise insipid mechanical existence will not be fit for humans and, this will cause human deterioration. Such apparently technical advancement will not replace human nature and can never be sustainable.

LOVE VS HATRED

Love: May there be peace for humans. They have me in their hearts and I could not have found a better abode. They are lovely. They help each other and, they are supreme.

Hatred: Don't you see the bloody battlefields and hear the crying? Don't they suffer at the hands of each other? They are each other's enemy. They want to hurt, kill and you say they are helping?

Love: I know you have smeared my image in the hearts of many. You deceived them and, they deviated from my way, but my image remains permanently in their hearts. I tell you that whenever they put off their selfishness, I will regain many.

Hatred: Selfishness is also my name and I put it in their minds. I have been tempting them to make themselves more secure and powerful by cheating, betraying, looting and killing others.

Love: Had they been faithful, they would have been more secure, but alas, many of them are not wise. Faith and sincerity are my names just as selfishness, deceit and wickedness are yours. Faith in One means unity, harmony, love, and faith will certainly overcome you.

Hatred: Don't you see that they have no faith in One, but separate religions. They hate plunder and even murder. I have made them believe that they do so in the name of the One although they do so in the name of religion and in the name of selfishness. Now many of them are not yours but mine, so you'd better concede your defeat.

Love: You are foolish to think so. Don't you see faithful lovely people?

Unselfish, loyal, sincere and having faith in the One? Tell me if you see any of your names in their hearts. Though they aren't many but, are spread over all parts of the world. How can any civilization exist without me? Many perish, where only you exist without my presence. Don't you need your existence? Do you want to die? I tell you that you are a parasite and feed on me. You came after I and, I was present before you in human hearts. If I weren't, there would be no humans left and all would perish and so would you.

Hatred: Do not be so angry. I want to live along with you, but I shall outnumber you as I already have been doing.

Love: I do not need your willingness. No doubt I shall live for more faithful and faithful never depart. You may betray many but, I never did betray any. I hope that humans will come back to their origin. You may outnumber, but you are frail. I am stronger in faith. You will perish before I and, deceit is frail. May humans always be human and leave their obstinacies of religion, caste, nation, selfishness, and regions. Such ignorance may be enlightened by me for I am love.

THE GOD GIVEN

Almost all religion holders say that everything is God or God's given, but most of them do not really believe this. To say it, customarily or traditionally and to have faith are different matters. Who-so-ever possesses wealth, health, power, honor, deems all such boon as his/her belongings. He takes such benefits as his personal capability, family inheritance or good luck. Very few take such blessings as the God given.

Had they taken such blessings as God given, they would have easily and naturally shared it with other humans who haven't. Haven't you witnessed that a father brings some things and gives to one of his children? He then wants the child to share those things with the other children, but the child refuses to share. Haven't you witnessed that some fellows want to search something in different ways? One of them happens to find something but denies other's share and argues that it was his/her good luck. There cannot be an equal distribution of all benefits and, humans have to live with many unjust inequalities. The God wants humans to work and live sensibly and with discretion. Factors like chance or luck also matter. Whatever the factors may be, the God, like a father, wants humans to take all benefits as blessings from the God and to be helpful, kind and loving to each other.

Humans do care and love their families and those who don't are not liked by the God. Who-so-ever lives carelessly, knowing that someone whom he may help is crying in pain, hunger or thirst, is a cruel person and the God hates the cruelty. The God wants every human to care for his family, neighbors, relatives, and friends. Sensible humans know who are the most deserving. No doubt charity begins at home but to provide basic-necessities of life to deserving humans is more liked by the God than to give luxuries to some.

Luxuries may never be a basis of happiness. If it were, the rich would never face depression. Basic necessities are a must and life may be lived happily without luxuries. Extravagance is not good and could be called selfish. The extravagant know that they are consuming unnecessarily that which could have been used to relieve suffering of deserving humanity. Misery is disgusting and is a form of cruelty. A miser is inhuman and is not liked by family, friends or common humans. He/she holds back when someone is in dire need of something. I believe that the extravagant and the miserly have no faith in the God and in the God's blessings.

Abuse of power by individuals and groups is a common vice among humans. When any group is more powerful than others; they want and attempt to usurp the other's freedom and rights. To remind others of their weakness and grab their freedom or due rights is also abuse of power. Had the powerful taken their power as God given, they would have been humble, kind to others and would have taken others' freedom as God given.

Those who believe that good health is also a blessing from the God must be kind and helping to the ill and disabled. Believers of the God never look down upon those who have less and are weaker in wealth, health or power. They may never be proud. They are humble, kind and loving to family, neighbors, relatives, friends and humanity.

UNIVERSAL HARMONIES

I am not a philosopher or a scientist, but I have some personal observations and feelings. I do not insist that my observations are correct, but I would like to write them down.

This universe is not static. The universe is very big and limitless so, our observations may not cover it. Planets are in constant motion. I think that there is a great harmony in all these movements. Whenever this harmony is broken there will be a great disaster and some religions may call it, "The Day of Judgment." No doubt when this harmony breaks there will be "The End." This harmonious universe and harmonious nature have direct impact on human lives. Let me call this harmony a melody or combination of various melodies. This melody is not heard by our hearing organs called "ears." When this harmony or melody is presented in melodious tunes, we hear it and it attracts our souls. When this melody is heard by loving hearts, they feel as being attracted towards their origin and there is a feeling of ecstasy.

I have observed that all movements by the living are naturally harmonious. I observe that a walking person's or a running horse's movements are naturally harmonious; even mechanical movements are harmonious. If movements of the living are intentionally broken, raised or slowed down and abruptly changed, we feel discomfort. If changes are gradual and harmony is not abruptly broken, there is no such discomfort. You can see that if a bus or train stops abruptly, a sleeping person will awaken quite disturbed. The sudden or abrupt change in motion may cause dangerous consequences physically, mentally or spiritually. There are also spiritual movements, not physical, which in case of any abrupt change may be harmful.

Classical melodies of any region are pleasure giving to all humans because they are melodious and are not abrupt. Abrupt sounds and voices are called noise, and those harmonious are melody. Humans have a common sense of harmonies and melodies. This sensibility is like other human values, so I say humans definitely have a common nature. This nature is God given and not at all accidental. Such common nature might not be accidental in all humans.

The harmonious melodies have an impact on the soul. Many people deny the very existence of soul. Melody is not a physical requirement. It is not food and it is not any physical attraction like that of males to females. It is attractive and, its attraction is certainly not for the body but for the soul. A human soul feels universal harmony and when it listens, like harmony produced through melody, it feels elevated from physical existence. It for the time being becomes a part of greater reality and although it has to come back to its physical requirement, it is comparatively raised up with broader vision.

There is a harmony more or, less in every human being. If this harmony is broken, the human feels anger, shallowness, hatred, depression and discontent. This may be called a disease of the soul, so it is not curable by physical treatment. Sincere love might be helpful, but faith in the God surely provides a sense of deep contentment and is a very certain remedy. Believers of the God certainly have great harmony of the soul. Human males and females have natural attraction for each other. Only this attraction may not be called love, but there might be love between such partners. If love exists they feel satisfaction and contentment. There are so many other aspects of love, love for all and love for humanity. Love is the basis of all sincere, unselfish human relations including blood relations, friends and humanity in general. Love is necessary for human life and love strengthens the harmony of the soul. Those who have faith in the God have lovely souls. No love, no faith. Faith does not co-exist with hatred and selfishness. It definitely inculcates many positive human values. Faith is love and love is the food of the soul.

TO MYSELF

Look, you feel something in your heart and you call it "faith."

Where did you get it? Have you earned it?

No. It isn't my achievement. I just meditated, thought about it and it was there, in my heart.

Is your heart a special one?

No. It is just the same as every other human heart.

Why then do you sometimes feel elevated over it?

Sometimes it just happens, or may happen, but I must not feel so. Whenever I feel such, I feel restlessness and my contentment, which my faith gives me, is lessened to some extent.

Why do you want people to know about your faith? Can't you keep silent?

I want to tell everybody. I am forced to keep silent; otherwise I would tell every human. I want to tell them it is such, it is faith, and it is in their hearts. I want to ask them whether they have it. If they answer, 'yes,' I shall ask them to compare with each other. Yes, it must be and, it must be the same, as we have like hearts. I see all living things want to live with their own species and, also search for them.

Why are you afraid when you claim that you have 'faith'?

I think that if I expose it to violent storms it may disappear before it is shown to those who may like to see. There may be a time that some would say, "Yes, it is like ours and ours is like it." If a time comes that I find no other way, I shall assert it vehemently in the face of storms and accept the God's will quite willingly.

Like most humans you are also entangled in affairs of life and you may seek favors for yourself in response to your faith. Would you, if time would favor you?

I seek the God's protection for it. I must not ever claim perfection. My faith is humble and, I may err. I know that I may not impart it to anyone if he/she is not inclined to believe, so I may not pass it on. It will be the God's blessing and not my endowment, so I must not seek any reward. May the God save me from any such wish!

Why don't you accept any religion, or become an atheist?

I strongly believe that the God is and is one and I cannot be an atheist. Religions attach compulsory ceremonies and manners which my faith does not accept. My belief is very simple. It may be everybody's without involving me or anybody else living or dead. I believe that the God is God of humans, God of all equally, not more of some, not less of some. Religious conditions fall heavily upon my heart. I will not surrender my freedom to these conditions. The God I believe is God of free humans and not of conditional bounds.

Why don't you ask your God to help you? You and your faith seem weak compared to religions and other believers.

I do seek the God's benevolence and help all the time. It is upon the God to decide. I must be content by His will. He is almighty, all knowing. I do not know what is good or not, should be or not. The God surely is just and my wishes might not be.

Why don't you then wait for the God's will, or continue your life like most humans without bothering about God, religion or faith?

Haven't you seen chirping birds at dawn or evening? They announce,

"There is the light, there is the light," or "Beware, the dark comes, the dark comes." They might be silenced for some time because of fear, but they resume as soon as it is over. It is very natural with them. The light or dark does not come for them only, but for all and all may see. The God I believe is not only mine, but of all, and all may feel; but just like birds, let me say, "The God is, the God is one, the God of the universe, the God of all. Feel the God."

IS IT THE SOUL?

Why feels lonely among many people.
Why is lost in the wilderness of the universe.
It looks through shut or open eyes,
In bustling daylight or in starry nights.

In nights much darkened by thick clouds,
Thundering, whistling or without sounds.
Rain or sun also many times takes it far,
As a journey-person of far and beyond.

Oceans, woods, valleys and in mountains
In far off lands and places beyond lands,
It wanders freely beyond boundaries false,
Why absorbs as it feels some unheard calls.

Why searches everywhere. What has it lost?
Is it the soul and seeks something of the past?

IF I WERE

If I were powerful enough, I perhaps would have humiliated my opponents,
Perhaps I would have dealt harshly with all those seemingly weak and powerless.
Thoughts of unjust dealings with humans would not have left me in peace.
Cruelty and wickedness certainly disturb a human heart. It's better not that I WERE.

If I were rich enough, perhaps I would have been living in luxury and quite selfish,
And needy humans would have suffered for something which I might have done,
Perhaps I would not have felt thirst and hunger, but satisfaction of being fed,
Perhaps I would not have felt hot or cold, but the blessings of shelter. It's better not that I WERE.

If I were poor enough, perhaps I would have lost the dignity of a human soul,
Perhaps I would have surrendered to any power other than the Almighty God,
Perhaps I would not have refuted evil allurements to meet crucial requirements,
Frailty is vulnerable and, faith is determination above doubt. It's better not that I WERE.

If I were free enough, perhaps I would not have thought any deep thought,
And therefore, would not have felt a sense of that sweet sadness in my soul,
Which mixed with a strong hope makes my faith, a faith in the merciful.
Perhaps I would not have been humble and submissive to the Lord. It's

better not that I WERE.

If I were born later, I might have seen that which I would not, or perhaps not seen.
If I were born before, I would have ended this life, would have certainly lost,
Many uncertainties, many would-haves, many 'perhaps' and many more thoughts.
No life without satisfaction, no faith without contentment, no to all IF I WERES.

Friends, it is a debatable matter that there is anything such as a "human soul." Almost all religions and, I also, believe that there is. I also believe that all human souls are alike and do not differ from time to time, region to region, race to race, religion to religion. Why then are there good and bad humans with so many differences including beliefs, behaviors and other views?

I believe that selfishness based on worldly attachments blur the human soul. Humans have different needs which make them selfish and the result is self-righteousness. Different sorts of selfishness cover the human soul to blur its originality. Let us sincerely think about such
differences. Let us restore originality of human souls. I do not claim that I have totally uncovered my soul, but I think that I have sincerely made efforts toward that purpose.

I believe that human souls if washed in pure waters of sincerity must compare with each other. Let us match souls. If they do not, some of us are in the wrong, or maybe all of us are. Let us remove blurriness. Let us uncover. Let us find that we are the same and the God created us humans. The human soul or you may say a human heart is God's abode. God's abode is not the places where we worship.

THE CHARM OF OBEDIENCE

Friends, we know that the wish to be obeyed is very common and charming. I have noticed that to obey is also a human characteristic. I have also observed that many animals willingly obey seniors of their kind and even their loving human masters. What I mean to say is that to obey is also natural and may be more pleasing than to be obeyed. Almost all religions claim obedience of the God but, every religion adds some necessary conditions without which obedience of the God is denied to willing humans.

The God almighty is worth obedience. None other deserves such obedience. He loves his humans so much more than parents love their children. If resemblance is to be mentioned then when parents love, obedience of children may be sighted. Many times, I have seen sensible children happily telling their friends that they were severely daunted by one or both of their parents or even beaten. That daunting or beating was certainly mixed with love which did not injure their feelings. Sometimes children may feel angry, but later-on they are much consoled, forget and most admit their fault. A baby does not know what is good for him so, parents teach him. Humans do not know what is good for them, so the God teaches, though sometimes He puts them under the test of loyalty, or, punishes them to put them on the right path.

Apart from minding parents, there is other willful obedience expected of humans which is religious. This is mainly traditionally dominated and obeyed by religious clergies, so-called fathers, gurus, and maulanas. Such tendencies also prove that there is a pervading spirit of obedience. Those who do not try to understand or, rise up to obedience of the God are entangled in such rules or, let me say, hindrances when they try to satisfy their instinct of obedience.

Friends, there may be such humans who really deserve obedience. They do not want to be obeyed and do not make efforts to be obeyed. Unlike religious leaders, they do not claim that their prayers will definitely work to fulfill wishes of concerned people. The wisdom of such persons is totally based on faith in the God. They do not claim to be an authority between humans and the God, so the people's obedience to them is totally unselfish. The only reason for such obedience is that their speech and deeds enhance the faith of people in the God so, those people feel the spirit of their compliance. Unlike religious, traditional obedience, or obedience of power, dominance, it is liked by the God as it ultimately serves the purpose of His bidding.

I do not want to mention qualities of such humans as the sensible are well-aware of good human characteristics. I only say that who-so-ever claims that he is inseparable of faith in the God and claims to provide any linkage between humans and God or, claims to know special manners or special prayers to please the God is definitely a hypocrite. The God of humans certainly listens to sincere callings of every human no matter to which religion he apparently belongs or does not belong at all.

Willing, unselfish obedience is a thing of great joy for the recipient which obedience by dominance or selfish reasons may not give. I believe the God created humans for their willing obedience and blessed them with free will for this purpose.

AN OUTLAW FACES THE DAY OF JUDGMENT

"Wake up. Don't you see that this is the court? We are all here to appear before the Almighty Lord. Haven't you got any company? Look, we are millions, billions. No, you can't count."

"He isn't from us. He is definitely lost. Perhaps he is not from a large company and minors are standing behind. Go and join the weak who are in the back. You may find your fellows there."

"He seems quite unconcerned, neither sad nor glad. Perhaps he is stunned as he sees big companies around."

"Look, no one allows him to join and he is not struggling to mix up. Pooh, the lonely, lazy person."

"Look, the ministers appear. Others have secured their places in front. You save your side. Oh, first of all they happen to meet him, the lonely one. He is caught up."

"Your majesties, he is neither from us nor from any other big company. We said grand prayers, held big ceremonies and made huge investments to please our God. Look, we are big."

"Not you, but we have been performing much better than you. We killed others and lost our lives to establish the God's command. Our holies and our laws are also the best ever given by the God to humanity. The God definitely prefers us."

"You are not right, and you shall see that we will definitely be awarded the first position. You and the others might be given yours subsequently."

"We are the major groups and the real contesters. Let this person be damned. He is wasting our time."

"Your majesties, none of us owns him. He is just an outlaw, an undisciplined person with no rule, no leader, no ceremonies, no authentic prayers and no certified manners. He is absolutely uncertified."

"Yes, majesties, he is just nothing, totally worthless and inconsiderable. None of us has any recommendation for him."

"Yes, ministers, they are right to say that I am an outlaw. They have been encouraging me to join any group, but I did not. Will you tell me which scale I was to use to measure the authenticity of their claims as each group, large or small, claims to be the sole representative of the God?"

"Majesties ask him if he has anything to present. He seems to be empty handed."

"I used to pray to my Lord in my heart, sometimes silently and sometimes in my words. Was I to learn special words and special language? I asked His favors very humbly, very sincerely and spontaneously as they came to my mind, not observing the sacred manners, uttering sacred words or observing sacred times in sacred places. Among the many faults I committed, there is sincerity in my heart. It might be hidden in my mistakes, but I am sure it is there. I want to present it to my Lord. It might be acceptable to Him."

"Oh, no, your majesties just get rid of him. He is creating a nuisance and very important groups like us are anxiously waiting for our rewards. He is a declared heathen, so no need of any jury. Just push him to Hell. How can he have any claim for Heaven with absolutely no performance?"

"All right, clear the way and let me proceed to Hell. I believe that my Lord is the Merciful and He will be giving me less punishment than I deserve. Thanks my Lord."

"Look how willingly and patiently he walks to Hell. He surely doesn't know what Hell means. He never learned such matters…poor ignorant man."

"My Lord, I have been bearing their taunts all my life and they ridicule me even now. I beg your mercy, but I never accepted and shall never accept anyone who intervenes between you and me. Just let me know that you want me to be in Hell and I shall refute all desires of Heaven. Bless my heart wherever I lay, I say to you, "The Merciful'."

"Who is it? Who invokes my mercy in such a pathetic tone? Stop him and bring him to me. If he approaches, all these claimants of Heaven will be thrown into Hell before he arrives."

"I am your Lord. I am the Merciful. I have seen your sincerity. Nothing remains hidden from me. Today is the Day of Judgment and only sincerity will be valued this day and not numbers or manner of prayers. Everybody is personally accountable and, no recommendations are acceptable…only sincerity. No group matters. I blessed every human with human values and every human will be responsible for self. Why did they not act upon it? Why did they obey devils? Why did they not follow the human nature which was engraved in every heart?"

"Sincerity, sincerity! Only sincerity! Have you any? Have you any? Have you any? Let us search in our hearts. No one can give it to anyone else."

"I am the Lord of every human. Bring the proud who claim to be interveners between me and my children and ask them what authority they had. They will be damned first of all. No one lies between me and a sincere human soul."

"Lord, give them severe punishment. They mislead many and claim that they will surely lead us to heaven. They also claim to be your agents."

"Yes Lord, they deserve a severe sentence. We were ordinary and they deceived us. Now they are denying any leadership."

SO-WHAT!

Friends, you certainly must have heard, 'so what!" Have you seen any person in an actual real condition of, 'so what' or experienced yourself a real, 'so what?' I mean, if a person loses his most dear through death – it might be his/her beloved or a child in case of parents, or any such loss, he might be in a condition of actual, 'so what'. Any other change or, incident, gain or loss, victory or defeat however large that might be, might seem to him/her, 'so what!' This state of 'so what' may be without any such loss or may not be even after many losses. That material gain or loss or seemingly deep suffering or achievement may be taken by a human as, 'so what'. You can try to tell him/her about his concerned group's gain or loss on a basis of race, nation or religion, but that means nothing to him/her. It does not necessarily mean that such a human is indifferent, unconcerned about his surroundings, but seemingly takes them as not very important.

I only want to say that a human may consider self above the temporary happenings of a temporary world; so we might understand the God not interfering in a direct visible manner regarding the injustices in this world (although I believe that the God surely responds to sincere calls or prayers and punishes the wicked or cruel). Certainly, you must have heard of a deplorable ending of life of some bad humans. You know, past is past. If a bad person having enjoyed so many years of life experiences a deplorable end, then those past years would mean to him/her, 'so what' as past has passed. If a good ordinary human who has lived so many years in a very ordinary manner or in some seemingly difficult conditions had a happy ending, then those past years would mean for such a human also, 'so what' as past had passed.

Sometimes suffering persons or groups do not seem to learn humbleness. Why don't they shake off all sorts of malice and evilness and resort to their creator with sincerity? I believe that if they learn to be humble, the God would be merciful to them. Why don't they feel mercy? If they learned to be merciful, the God would surely be merciful to them. None of these worldly attainments, riches, power, health, may be taken as full requirements of a human life. A spiritualistic approach is required to properly understand the blessing of the God.

YEARNINGS OF A SOUL

It is a debatable matter whether or, not there is a soul. If there is a soul then, there is something more lasting than apparent physical existence. That 'more-lasting' time may be everlasting. If there is presence of a soul, then let me say there is a spirit, a creator, the God. Let us consider the yearnings of a soul which transcends material requirements and physical existence.

Humans enjoy music or, are attracted to melodious sounds and voices. A violin cord is played, or a flute is blown. They touch our hearts and we feel attracted towards an invisible object. Such feelings of attraction are not the same in all humans. Some feel a sense of ecstasy and some are not very moved, but we all know that the effect exists. Can we prove scientifically or physically that such effects are no doubt a reality? Melodies may not be taken as a physical requirement, or you may say, 'the need of the flesh'. Does it mean that there is nothing else besides our flesh or physical existence?

I have observed that non-musical humans are often insensitive and materialistic. They also lack aesthetic sense. Such commercialism breeds impatience, restlessness and no doubt, deprives some humans of real happiness and pleasure. Such humans might get possible materialistic and physical pleasures but lack the pleasure which esthetic humans feel in the charm of melodies. Such lack of real pleasures may plunge them into depression which material tools may not heal.
A great and original melody exists in human hearts so, it responds to outward melodies. Responding humans are naturally loving, kind, humane and spiritualistic. They may or may not get rich, but live a contented life and unlike others, do not feel restless or impatient to compete in material belongings.

It is not necessary to hear melodies produced by worldly instruments as the responding humans may feel it in the universe (illustrated in the article, "Universal Harmonies"), I imagine you have seen any human so absorbed that for that time becomes unconscious of his surroundings. That human is often alone, but not necessarily; may not be remembering a past or engaged in future planning, yet for the time being is detached from the present. Such absorption is of the soul and not concerned with the physical world. This is the reason that monks dwell in lonely places, in mountains and woods, on riverbanks or seaside. This practice also can become a ritual, traditional or ceremonial. I think it is not necessary to live apart for such absorption and those who live in society may even better fulfill such yearnings of the soul. I hope you understand and, also feel what I am saying. Is it not the soul which absorbs and seeks such yearnings? Do you think this is a physical requirement?

Maybe you have noticed or felt that humans may desire to be sad and even to weep. They may like to read sad stories, sing sad songs, and even witness sad events. They do not want such events to happen, but if they are experienced or witnessed, they feel a sort of purification. Sad songs are sung or enjoyed by those who may never have had any sadness in their lives. They may yearn for such sadness more than humor. Laughing is not bad, but it is not necessarily from joy or pleasure. Joy or pleasure is of a lasting nature which jokes may not provide. Joy is not a result of materialistic belongings although basic requirements of food and shelter, or gratification of masculinity or femininity may be necessary. Joy is love, love of any human relation or friend. Joy is fulfillment of the yearnings of the soul and not a physical need. Why do humans sometimes yearn to be sad?

I think that a human soul possesses an inborn hidden desire to elevate itself from physical bindings. This desire is stimulated by harmonious melodies sad or not, heard or unheard. When such a desire overwhelms a soul, it feels a sort of sadness as it feels itself unable to fly to an unknown far off destination beyond the horizon, beyond skies.

It does not mean that such yearnings may result in an unnatural self-breaking life circle. Suicide is an outcome of failure of materialistic desires and wishes. It may be an outcome of negative moral boosting of the insensible by the insensitive. Will a good human kill his fellow if the latter desires him to do so? Can such a killing be justified? If not, then why is self-killing allowed by the God or by good humans? Life is not a personal matter as it may never be produced or created but by the God only. To kill one's self is to kill a human.

Aesthetic sadness and depression are separate things and have nothing to do with each other. Humor is not bad, but even the humorous may plunge into a deep depression ending in self-breaking of his life cycle. Harmonious humans irrespective of their apparent religions are tender, gentle, loving, enduring and deeply patient. They may have a sense of wit. They do have a harmony of soul, a well-balanced sense of life. Perhaps in science it is called a balanced mind, but science may never define it properly. It is more concerned with spirituality than science otherwise all physicians would be better humans than others. Humans should understand yearnings of the soul as it is the natural way to live a balanced, satisfied and contented life. Spirituality realizes aspirations and yearnings of the soul and it is not a religion.

My mystic poet says,
"Break mosque (Muslim's worship place), mender (Hindu's worship place) (two major religious groups of the Indian sub-continent) and break whatever you may, but do not break a human heart – the God resides within."

A STRANGER

Why play strange music though sweet and melodious,
To distract from established rules is always hazardous?
Why sing strange songs though lovely and attractive,
May you keep silent as freedom may be dangerous?

Why like a ripened fruit draw attention of pickers,
Or like laden clouds set to shed heavy burdens,
Or like a thirsty traveler in desolate rough lands,
You tend to drink that which might be poisonous?

Have you faith to jump into vast and awful waters,
To take you to a destination which might be perilous?

DOES NOT RECOGNIZE THE GOD

May be poor but does not feel poverty.
May be helpless but does not feel helplessness.
May be hungry but does not feel hunger.
May be without shelter but does not feel shelter less.

May be thirsty but does not feel thirst.
May be alone but does not feel loneliness.
May be quarrelsome and does not feel love.
May not be powerful but does not feel powerless.

May be in trouble but does not feel patience.
May be dignified but does not feel meek.
May be opposed but does not feel mercy.
May be healthy but does not feel illness.

May be right but does not feel another's right.
May be brave but does not feel tenderness.

RECOGNIZES THE GOD

May be poor but does not yearn for luxuries.
May be wise but trusts only in the God's will.
May be grieved but does not go beyond peaceful sadness.
May be annoyed but keeps in touch with love.

May be blessed but does not take as self-achievement.
May be simple but is not foolish.
May be punishing but does not exceed justice.
May be prudent but is not a miser.

May be joyous but does not forget sufferings.
May be having but is not a boaster.

THE CREATOR OF THE UNIVERSE

I believe that the God is the sole and absolute creator and controller of the universe. I believe that every human who has attained the age of sensibility may obtain such a belief through personal inclination, pondering, experience and meditation. Such humans may be anybody anywhere in the world. There are religious, traditional and ceremonial beliefs or so-called beliefs without any personal inclination or meditation. How can faith in the God be collective if an individual does not bother about it? Is not every human responsible for his own deeds and faith? However, collectiveness is good if the participants are sincere and understand the grounds of their participation.

I think traditional beliefs are losing viability to the so-called modern scientific approach. However, mankind is naturally inclined to have a belief in an unseen power though their naturalness is defiled and they are misguided by self-righteous religious clergies. Sincere wise humans can and may be led to a true sincere faith.

Humans take everything which they are used to seeing or experiencing as a routine matter, or a scientific process. For example, had there been no sleep and, a human happens to have sleep and rise again, they would have taken it as a miracle. Had there been no tornadoes and they happened to see one, they would have taken it as a miracle, or a warning from an unseen power. Similarly had there been no earthquakes, volcanoes or other disaster, they would have observed, paid attention to and contemplated them.

Humans know about the vastness of the universe, but its vastness is not within our imagination and can never be…it has an unimaginable vastness, unimaginable number of planets and stars. Do humans know about its perfection? If even one of them slips from its place, it might cause unimaginable destruction -- perhaps total and absolute. Perhaps science says it is all accidental and by chance. What an unimaginable, unlimited and unbelievable chance without any creator or controller! Every one of these innumerable stars and planets is keeping its place, pace and continuity with perfect harmony.

Humans know that there is life on one planet called Earth. It is placed in the universe in such a locale perfectly and delicately that it may not have any symptoms of life if, it weren't in such an exact position. Night falls, sun rises and, we count days and years. Weather changes and there is an indispensable water cycle; so many and various factors which are necessary for life. Even one other of these has never been found to be present anywhere else in this vastness of the universe. So many creatures and plants, so different and alike; and mankind has been benefiting from many of them. Was all that by chance? We know some scientists have strived to solve the mystery. Alas! They do not contemplate sensibly. It is not and may not be within their reach. Mystic's meditation may understand and solve it, but not the so-called scientists. Life itself, its creation, reproduction and everything around us are miracles of the God and nothing else. Just imagine what would happen if Earth absorbs the waters of the oceans and takes it to its inner depths.

Humans do not understand the blessings which they all have in general. They take them as a common routine and do not bother to contemplate on them. They wish for anything special for a particular group or. person in order to be thankful to the God, or to take as a miracle.

Scientific progress by humans is also the God's will. He certainly channeled humanity to achieve scientific progress at a fixed time; otherwise humans were not of inferior capabilities hundreds or thousands of years ago. This progress is certainly not without any purpose as nothing happens without any purpose or without the God's will. The God knows what the purpose might be. I think there might be a great change in the future. No one can predict what kind of change it might be. One purpose it is serving is that people including me are communicating with each other through the internet; otherwise, I would have been blocked in a small sphere of rigidity. Thanks to God I take it as a blessing and let me say that I also take it as a miracle of the God.

MINISTERS, JINN AND DEVILS

There are said to be some creatures acting on behalf of the God. In some religions such ministers are called angels and in some, deities. Why does the God, being the Almighty, require such ministers when He can do whatever He likes within no time and without any effort?

The God created humans with free will so He might have created such a being that may not disobey him, be absolutely loyal and obedient. Such ministers may not be deputies, assistants and not at all helpers as it would interfere with His entirety, absolute universal domain. Any faith in God dependent on others for any sort of execution would be quite unnatural and so unacceptable for true faithful humans. They might be executing some assignments absolutely in accordance with the God's will but may not be respondents to any calls or prayers. They may not act on their own, so why prayers and why calls?

The God does not allow any sort of sharing of his powers and prayers. It is totally unnatural to believe in a god or gods sharing the power. The God created humans in his own image.

Are there or are there not, how many and what are the names of such ministers have no concern with faith in the God? How can humans who happen to live in different regions of the world know about such matters? All religions differ on many issues. Such issues are totally unnecessary additions and true faith consists of only ONE, the Almighty, the God. The God might have created creatures for appearance in any shape, for any purpose at anytime, anywhere and in any number, but faith in the God is not at all inclusive of any additional compulsions. If there are ministers or angels, then they are good fellows doing good always without any possibility of error or fault.

There is said to be an invisible creation called jinn and perhaps devils are also of their tribe. Jinn may be good or bad, but devils are the symbol of evil. It is also believed that there is one chief devil, Satan, the absolute evil who entices humans to selfishness and evil deeds and diverts them from the straight path to the God and goodness.

Strife between good and evil is said to be on-going. Such strife may be within every human. Goodness demands humans to overpower or get rid of evil and evil has its allurements. Evil is based on selfishness in humans so, they are cruel, cowardly and extravagant, miserly and wicked. Such selfishness is based on self-projection, self-promotion or as they think, self-protection, though they do not actually achieve these objectives through such evil.

If evil and good exist to attract humans to their side, then evil is no doubt the biggest enemy of all humans and deserves the most severe condemnation. Such condemnation also becomes necessary to get the favor of goodness. Protection of the Almighty is no doubt the most reliable shelter, so it should be sought and prayed for to suppress evil allurements and to overcome the forces of evil. May be devil/devils or not, is also not an issue of importance with-regard to faith in God.

If magic exists then it reflects harmony instead of discord between humans and devils. Such humans show their loyalty to evil and, whoever are steadfast and persistent are more successful evildoers or magicians. They denounce good and the God. They are truly damned regardless of their creed attachment. They seek help from devils instead of the God.

True believers of the God who seek guidance, forgiveness and protection from the God need not worry about jinn or devils as they may not harm them, but those obstinate who persistently defy goodness may be their victims. True believers do not seek help from evil forces in whatever situation they may be. The God is Almighty and absolutely worthy of all possible trusts; so why fear other forces if there are any. Faith in the God does not include any particular-belief about any such forces and believers may remain unconcerned. However, I feel the presence of such unseen deluding elements diverting me from the right path and spirituality. Damned elements or persons wish and like others to be damned.

Sincerity of a relationship is not lessened but deepened and intensified even, it faces severe condemnation or hardship. Do not most humans have other objectives or supplementary objectives in-order to have a relationship or to have faith in the God? Do they not want the God to accept their wishes, likings and inherited or chosen ways as the only possible truth instead of asking the God for guidance? Do they not need to look closely into their hearts if they claim sincerity in their relationship with the God?

LET US SAY LOVE PRAYERS

My mystic poet says,
"Those who say love prayers do not open and read Koran (holy book of Muslims)."

Friends, do you know the difference between love prayers, those ceremonial or religious prayers? Is the God universal or religious? What ceremonies does the God like if religious?

I think love emanates from the heart and overpowers the mind. In its direction, it sweeps over barren rationality. Love is happiness which material joys may not provide and, is a main characteristic of spiritual existence beyond physical life. Strong love often overflows like a flood, so there may not be any settled order or laws for its manifestation. Unlike traditions, or religion, pure love is never ceremonial. Love is a passion which does not take into consideration any reward or return.

Those who are of a loving nature love all; love all human relations including friends, the needy, week and humanity in general They are not cruel even to animals. Love makes sacrifices. A materialistic attitude in humans is anti-faith and anti-spirituality. Those who remain engrossed in commercialism disregard the sufferings of the needy. Those who do not feel love are actually not humans but, human animals. Extravagance is also an outcome of materialistic and commercial inclination. Love is a natural instinct so, it likes to dwell in a simple and natural atmosphere rather than in artificial, superficial and luxurious.

Can sincere love be ceremonial? Can it be put under administrative control? Can lovers be taught manners, times and behavior to love? Can emotions be certified like academic knowledge? Can heart-felt passion be confined to repetition of particular religious words?

Just like all other occupations, love is the God-gifted virtue of lovers. They know how to spread love, and the task may not be assigned to non-lovers and hypocrites. They naturally know how to say love prayers without bothering and without considering so-called sacred manners or words. Whatever words they use, whatever language they speak, or say silently without any words and without any language are love prayers. Let there be no interference between a lover and a beloved. Love is the joy of lovers and beloveds and, to put hindrances in between is totally unjustified and sheer vindictiveness. Can torrential rains and other functions of nature be brought under desired limitations? I am sure you will say, 'no'. Why then are lovers asked to say prescribed or approved prayers? Love is as vast as the universe and so are love prayers.

Why do most people not hear the call of nature and stubbornly insist on their wishful beliefs? It clearly says, "There is a God, the God is one, the God of the universe is equally the God of all humans and not of religious groups or communities. Nature came into being from love and for love. Selfishness divides humans and they claim superiority over one another in the name of God. This is too bad, unjustified and is very often a base of hatred. Let us love. Let us say love prayers.

Lord, I am I, the lonely traveler,
Your people shut their doors to me,
They say they may accept me,
If I accept their authorities of endorsement,
For being eligible to have a faith in you,
I have come to you refusing all authorities,
If you accept me I get all the blessings I need,
If you want me to wait, grant me patience,
To stay at your door in rain or shine,
Let me be yours, let me not be of any else.

My mystic poet says, "Hajjis (Muslim pilgrimages) go to Mecca. I shall go to Takhat Hazara (home town of hero and lover of a renowned folk love story of Punjab). He, imagining himself as Heer (hero) says, 'Where my friend resides, there is my Mecca'. Actually he was lover of the God."

Friends, did you imagine that even lovers of love stories in the east or west were better humans as compared ;to most others? Yes, sincere love softens hearts and love for the Creator makes humans the supreme creation.

DEPRESSION

Like all other living beings, human basic- necessities are food, shelter and coupling, productive or not. If the basic necessities are available and met with, they tend to engage themselves in different ways. These encumbrances may or may not give them pleasure but are necessary to allow them to become part of the on going process of time and life. Anger, hatred, jealously and enmity may not give real pleasure, but even such negative values provide a kind of involvement and any kind of stumbling block keeps depression away.

Modes of awkwardness change under different conditions and circumstances. An embarrassing situation may provide a poor person a great joy, but another may take that as just capriciousness. For some persons a meaningful relationship may be new or joyous and, for some old or weary. Some are enamored of wealth or luxuries, some power, some reputation, some by honor or so-called honor and some take pride in other things. Religious, traditional and cultural connections are also of much importance as they keep people engaged and provide necessary hope.

Sincere relationship with other humans is the most important factor. There are few chances of sincere human involvement without taking family into account. A family life with all its aspects of relatives and sincere friends are very effective help against depression. These may differ with similar conditions and circumstances. A person may be involved in natural beauty and another may not, or a person may be involved in one kind of pleasure and the other not.

Being connected with others is a must to be free of depression and, its degree does not depend on materials or riches. This deeper degree of involvement means there is less probability of depression. Any seemingly worthless situation is replaced by another valuable one and life goes on. If this circle breaks, depression takes over. People are always involved in changes productive and positive, negative and destructive. If there is a big change affecting many or attracting public interest it is called news. Besides this there are personal, family, local and regional changes which keep concerned persons involved. In-fact people do not want time or life static as it is against nature although, change inevitably takes them to an end called death. If change is desirable, they feel happy for the time being and if it is undesirable, they feel dejected or may get depressed.

A spiritualistic vision provides the most reliable and unbreakable source of involvement. It does not negate other true pleasure giving but, enhances the degree with deeper sensitivity and emotion. It is based on love so, it attracts love but relies on faith in the God. It does not lose satisfaction and contentment if left alone because, spirituality derives its nourishment from nature. No doubt connection with other humans is worth more than any other materialistic possession. A modern materialistic way of life has deprived humans of some natural participation in life. Moreover, if non-believers truly and deeply understand the meaning of death, they are much more likely to be overwhelmed by depression. True faith in the God provides the deepest hope and contentment which any sort of materialistic failure may not break. Love humanity and have faith in the God irrespective of any religious, racial or regional attachment in-order-to enjoy life peacefully in its pure sense.

Depression is starvation of natural human instincts and emotions. In uncivilized societies it is most likely to be as-a-result of suppression but, generally the affected persons do not acknowledge and deny any sort of suffering from starvation and, often become psychological cases. If the affected person is wise enough to acknowledge his starvation for human contact, the rescue becomes easy, but in all cases sincerity and manifestation of sincerity is necessary by attached persons. Spirituality has a very wide scope for freedom to let off emotions, so it provides sound relief.

HEAVEN AND HELL

The God created humans to individually prove their sincerity with Him on a scale accepted in the face of many selfish temptations. Humans may fail to do so and, failure of any sort is also graded. When this process is completed in the shape of death or an ultimate huge disaster, there has-to be some reward or punishment worthy of the Almighty's authority. The trial period is not always long and may never continue until it ends forever.

Mostly there is equilibrium in the relationship of two or more concerned sides. They may equal in sincerity but, there may not be any human who can compare with the Almighty's love for him or her. No one knows what scale of judgment the Almighty would be using. No doubt he is the merciful; so there would be as great forgiveness as befitting his greatness but the cruel and wicked may not be eligible of his love.

Once a person is forgiven may not have any fear of facing fate. Once forgiven, would not experience any negative human values such as greed, jealousy or hatred. Being responsive to His pardon, the person would be forever grateful to the Lord. As the trial period would have been over, there would be no allurements to distract any human. There may not be any unfulfilled, ungratified desires as that would be against the full contentment of blessed humans and, the Almighty would like their complete gratefulness. All desires would be gratified to fullest extent imaginable. All tastes and comforts which humans can conceive will have no possibility of ending. There would not be full gratification if, there were any time restrictions, however remote and far distant they might be. It would have to be everlasting. Such a place of blessings may be called Heaven. Heaven and its blessings have-to be limitless for the fullest pleasure. Also, there may be people more deserving of blessings.

No one can judge the level of His forgiveness so, no one can know how much punishment would be awarded to condemned persons. It would have to be different for all individuals. Perhaps all would see horrors and awfulness of the place called Hell. Those who would be forgiven would imagine the horrors and would be very grateful for mercy of the God. Perhaps those who were very cruel and stubborn would suffer punishment before consideration for forgiveness. As blessings of heaven would be beyond imagination, the horrors of Hell would be also. The cruel and stubborn would panic, be baffled and frightened. They would not have experienced such plight ever before.

I believe that every human has a sense/feeling of eternity and, without achieving it may never be fully satisfied/contended. There would be a time of Judgment; there would be rewards and punishment which, can be imagined by believers so, no particular-defined explanations are necessary. Hope and trust in His mercy and love are all, they need.

SOME THOUGHTS AND OBSERVATIONS

Fear the God but, have faith in His love and mercy.

The land you live on has taken in your innumerable generations but, do not lose heart and feel the eternity in yourself.

Have faith in the God but without meditation and understanding it is superfluous.

Help those who ask for it but, some not asking may deserve priority.

Aggression is bad but, not defending the just and innocent if, one has the capability to do so is worse.

Be not impatient for any achievement. Its invisible bad may be greater than its visible good.

Thank the God for His blessings upon you and, do not be ungrateful by comparing them with others.

Love your land and people but, be willing to leave them for any just or noble cause.

Be ever ready to discuss, rethink and reconsider your faith with full flexibility if, you are confident of its reliability.

The God is as much yours as He may be of anybody else. Your heart is the God's abode; just clear it of all pre-occupation based on religion, race, region, economics and tradition and make it a pure human heart.

Sometimes weeping provides better relief than laughing.

No doubt freedom is good for all humans but, sometimes suppression raises better humans than freedom can.

Just as sincere friends share joys and sorrows, believers thank the God for blessings and, ask for relief from suffering for themselves and others. People call it prayer.

Very strange, but people often wish other's deprivation in-order to feel lucky even though, it does not benefit them.

Why do humans not become inhuman? Why care for principle and sacrifice pleasures for others? Why care for any change after death however great it may be if there isn't any soul?

Free your thoughts and you are, "Out of religion." Meditate on the universe and nature and you are, "In Spirituality."

Most people are inclined to believe what they like to believe and, are not inclined to believe what they do not want to believe. This is also bigotry.

Pray to the God in sadness and gladness in a peaceful state of mind. Anger, impatience, pride and depression damage the inner peace of soul and prayers.

The Creator equally loves all humans but, when they become selfish, claim preference over each other and, do not recognize Him as the common creator of all, they create hatred.

Broken-hearted calls at difficult times by believers are most likely to get prompt response. Their intensity and depth of passion attracts the kindness and mercy of the God.

The God likes those who realize another's good more than their own and, analyze self-weaknesses more than the others.

Realizing and analyzing self-weaknesses, failures and mistakes surely make humans wise but, the unwise do not have the flexibility to undergo such process.

Good is universal. Selfish people create personal, regional and communal goods and, their so-called goods clash with other's goods. Good never differs from good.

Though it is odd people do not wish to grow old but, wish their babies to grow young.

Friendship is not a deal. Sincere friends do not take advantage of their relationship. Sincerity has no agreements or laws.

Wisdom is ignorance in an unwise society.

Do not blame the God if, anyone claims His attorney has some personal weaknesses or, any book attributed to Him contains some flaws. He blessed you with human values, all good is Godly and all bad un-Godly.

Be quick to ask forgiveness from the weak even for minor wrongs, the God likes it. To ask forgiveness from the mighty is a different matter.

No doubt truth is good but, a lie which saves the innocent from cruelty is better than a heartless truth; although such occasions are very rare.

Contentment is a state of the soul which, material possessions or achievements cannot provide however great they may be.

A loving heart is essential and the only eligibility to have faith in the God. Those who do not qualify need not seek it in books or prayers.

Wisdom is ability and ignorance inability to acknowledge and accept the truth.

Religions consist of allowed or not allowed and, not necessarily good or truthful, while faith in the God naturally recognized universal good and truth.

Whosoever seeks finds the God, but religions deny this inborn equal right of humans and each religion claims to be an exclusive permit holder.

Unlike religions, faith in the God is neither a heritage nor an inheritance.

www.ingramcontent.com/pod-product-compliance
Lightning Source LLC
Chambersburg PA
CBHW030322080526
44584CB00012B/666